Translating H/holy S/spirit

4 Models: Unitarian, Binitarian, Trinitarian, and Non-Sectarian

Garrett C. Kenney

University Press of America,® Inc.
Lanham · Boulder · New York · Toronto · Plymouth, UK

Copyright © 2007 by
University Press of America,® Inc.
4501 Forbes Boulevard
Suite 200
Lanham, Maryland 20706
UPA Acquisitions Department (301) 459-3366

Estover Road
Plymouth PL6 7PY
United Kingdom

All rights reserved
Printed in the United States of America
British Library Cataloging in Publication Information Available

Library of Congress Control Number: 2006934335
ISBN-13: 978-0-7618-3645-2 (paperback : alk. paper)
ISBN-10: 0-7618-3645-4 (paperback : alk. paper)

∞™ The paper used in this publication meets the minimum
requirements of American National Standard for Information
Sciences—Permanence of Paper for Printed Library Materials,
ANSI Z39.48—1984

Dedication

To

Mike Snell and Pat Hurley

Contents

List of Abbreviations for Bible Translations	ix
Preface	xi
The Four Models	xiii
Introduction	**xv-xix**
Initial Questions and Overview	xv
Necessary Distinctions; Basic Terminology; a Few Statistics;	
and Foundational Definitions	xvi
3 Distinct Usages	xvii
Notes	xviii
Chapter One: Preliminary Illustrations:	**1-17**
Genesis 1:2	1
Genesis 3:8	2
Genesis 6:3	2
Genesis 41:8	3
Genesis 41:38	3
Exodus 28:3 and 31:3	4
Numbers 11: 16-17 and 25-31	5
Psalm 51:9-12	7
Isaiah 11:1-2	8
Isaiah 40:13 & 1 Corinthians 2:16	9
Isaiah 48:16	11
Isaiah 63: 9-11	12
Ezekiel 36:26-27	13
Key Issues and Tensions	14
Notes	17
Chapter Two: The Unitarian Model	**19-36**
A Brief Summary of the Unitarian Position	19
An Expansion of the Above Arguments	20-33
The unambiguous declaration that there is one God,	
the Father	20
Ephesians 4:4-6	21
John 17:5	22
1 Corinthians 8:6	22

Apparent affirmations of the deity of the Son	24
Mark 10:18	24
Mark 13:32	25
John 6:38	25
John 16:13	25
"The God and Father of our Lord Jesus Christ"	26
The title "God"	27
The absence of prayer and/or worship directed to the Holy Spirit	27
Acts 8: 9-25	27
Absence of any polemic regarding the deity of the Spirit	29
Passages which appear to present the Spirit as a separate Person and/or equal in deity to the Father and/or Son	29
Ephesians 4:30	30
Matthew 28: 19	30
Matthew 3:11 and Luke 3:15	32
2 Corinthians 13:14	32
Notes	33
Chapter Three: The Binitarian Model	**37-50**
A Brief Summary of the Binitarian Position	37
An Expansion of the Above Arguments	38-48
Binitarian Formulas	38
Proverbs 8:22-23; Colossians 1:15; Revelation 3:14	38
John 1:18	39
Hebrews 1:1-2	40
Early Christian Worship	42
The Spirit in Binitarianism	43
The Paraclete of John's Gospel.	44
Notes	48
Chapter Four: The Trinitarian Model	**51-58**
A Brief Summary of the Trinitarian Position	51
An Expansion of the Above Arguments	52-57
The Spirit as a Distinct, Divine Person	52
The Spirit as the New and Effective Revealer of God	54
The Spirit and Religious Experience	55
The Spirit as the Principle of Union	56
Notes	57
Chapter Five: The Non-Sectarian Model	**59-64**
A Brief Summary of the Non-Sectarian Position	59

Contents vii

An Expansion of the Above Arguments	60-63
Unitarianism	60
Binitarianism	61
Trinitarianism	61
A Reiteration of the Non-Sectarian Position	63
Notes	63
Conclusion	**65**
Illustrations	**67-72**
God as Father	67
The Unitarian Model	69
The Binitarian Model	70
The Trinitarian Model	71
Personification and Hypostatization	72
Bibliography	**73-75**
Author Index	**77**
Scripture Index	**79-83**
About the Author	**85**

Abbreviations for Bible Translations

(all these versions were accessed from internet site: http:www.keyverse.com with the exception of the *New English Bible*)

ASV	American Standard Version
AMP	Amplified Bible
BBE	Bible in Basic English
CEV	Contemporary English Version
CSV	Christian Standard Version
DB	Darby Bible
DR	Douay Rheims Translation
ESV	English Standard Version
GNT	Good News Translation
JPS	Jewish Publication Society
KJV	King James Authorized Version
KJ21	King James 21st Century
MSG	The Message
NAB	New American Bible
NASB	New American Standard Version
NEB	New English Bible
NIV	New International Version
NKJV	New King James Version
NLT	New Living Translation
NRSV	New Revised Standard Version
RSV	Revised Standard Version
WB	Webster's Bible
WEB	World English Bible
WNT	Weymouth New Testament
YLT	Young's Literal Translation

Preface

This book represents a quest for understanding the concept of the Holy Spirit in the Christian tradition. On the next page, Four Models of the Holy Spirit are presented. The Introduction provides necessary distinctions, basic terminology, some statistics, foundational definitions, and an explanation of three usages. Chapter One provides some preliminary illustrations. Chapters 2-3-4 and 5 present a defense of each of the Four Models. The Conclusion reflects back upon this study.

As a Christian, I have been a member of Unitarian and Trinitarian religious communities. As a scholar, I have at times entertained the notion that the best explanation is to be found in Binitarianism and/or Non-Sectarianism. My motivation for writing this book was to share my soul searching and scripture searching with interested readers.

The design of this book, presenting Four Models in a positive and sequential fashion, drew inspiration from several other studies utilizing a four or several model approach. Some that come to mind are: *4 Views on Hell: Literal; Metaphorical; Purgatorial; and Conditional* (1992); *The Meaning of the Millennium 4 Views* (1977: Historic Pre-millennialism; Dispensational Pre-millennialism; Postmillennialism; and Amillennialism). *Divine Foreknowledge 4 Views* (2001: Open Theism; Simple-Foreknowledge; Middle-Foreknowledge; and The Augustinian-Calvinist View), and *The Construction of Orthodoxy and Heresy: Neo-Confucian, Islamic, Jewish, and Early Christian Patterns* (1998). There are many other texts like these. Most of them have a common and helpful feature, sadly missing in my volume. Most of the books designed like this are the result of a collaboration and dialogue among different scholars representing the various views, each scholar interacting with the others in "response-chapters." This book could have benefited from the work of several minds and the help of an editor. Who knows, maybe it will inspire such a needed collaboration. Nevertheless, I think I have provided a start in that direction and would be a willing participant in such an endeavor.

I end this preface with a quote by John Hinnels, editor of the *Dictionary of Religions* (1995), as it aptly expresses the importance of my subject. With regard to the concept of Spirit, Hinnels states: "The singular concept defies definition. Denoting the form of being which has no distinctly material properties, 'spirit' (derived like its equivalents in many languages from words for breath or wind, as invisible, yet powerful and life-giving), connotes life, consciousness, self-activity. Religion is often regarded as having to do with 'the things of the spirit', what is spiritual. To elucidate such language is a major task for Religionswissenshaft and the Philosophy of Religion" (492-93).

Garry Kenney
Spokane, Washington
June 1, 2006

The Four Models

(1): Unitarian: The Godhead is one in substance, one in person, namely, the Father. When capitalized, "Holy Spirit" is a synonym or metonym for God the Father. When lower case, "holy spirit" refers to some attribute or action of God in manifestation in creation or within the human spirit and thus is understood as an impersonal power, influence, or gift.

(2): Binitarian: The Godhead is one in substance, two in persons, Father and Son. The same distinctions regarding "Holy Spirit" and "holy spirit" mentioned above are applicable in this model. Binitarians argue that "spirit" sometimes "represents" or may be understood as a "personification" of the union of the Father and the Son.

(3): Trinitarian: The Godhead is one in substance, three in persons, Father, Son, and Holy Spirit. The "Holy Spirit" refers to the Third Person of the triune Godhead.

(4): Non-sectarian: This view sets aside any particular understanding of the Godhead. God-talk in the biblical tradition is inconsistent and does not allow for such clarity. No confessional option is to be recommended over another. Unitarianism, Binitarianism, and Trinitarianism are "paradigms of convenience" for the religious communities that adopt them. They simply provide adherents with a way to image or understand God. The biblical occurrences of "Holy Spirit" and/or "holy spirit" are too inconsistent and too ambiguous to allow for any confessional precision.

Introduction

Initial Questions and Overview

Have you ever wondered who or what the H/holy S/spirit is? Have you ever wondered why Bible translators randomly oscillate between capitalizing and lower casing S/spirit? Have you ever wondered about the Trinity? When, why, and how did this doctrine originate? What exactly is the Trinity? Is it the best or most preferred explanation for the relevant data of scripture and tradition? This study ponders these and similar questions. As you read this treatise on H/holy S/spirit my hope is that the above questions will be brought into focus and that some satisfying answers or insights will emerge. Please read my treatise patiently and thoughtfully. My aim has been to provide thoughtful reflection for adherents of all the views discussed. Ecumenism is important. And, so is the truth.

This study presents four models for understanding the concept of the Holy Spirit/holy spirit in the Judeo-Christian tradition. When I capitalize "Holy Spirit," I intend the reader to think of a person.[1] Two options present themselves here. In the first case, "Holy Spirit" may simply function as a synonym (a term of similar or identical meaning) or as a metonym (substitute term) for God the Father. Secondly, "Holy Spirit" may be interpreted to refer to the "Third Person" of the Trinity. When I lower case "holy spirit," I intend the reader to think of a God-given but impersonal force, power, capacity, or gift. Again, two options present themselves here: In the first case, "holy spirit" represents a way of speaking about God in His immanent/visible manifestations and/or interactions with creation and/or creatures. Secondly, "holy spirit" may refer to God's gift(s) of grace, some enablement or capacity within the human spirit for spiritual service, or even to indicate a new nature within the human person, which upon receipt, may be understood as the possession of the recipient. In other words, "holy spirit" may be a way of speaking of the human spirit in a sanctified or empowered state. Often I will employ both forms (Holy Spirit/holy spirit; or more frequently, S/spirit) thus emphasizing for the reader the interpretive problem.

The four models, Unitarian, Binitarian, Trinitarian, and Non-Sectarian are presented in this order because this is the historical order in which the models developed. Each model is presented as positively and persuasively as my abilities permit. Each model is also scrutinized for weaknesses or inconsistencies. Prior to developing each model, I orient the reader by providing the following:

In the Introduction-a) initial questions and overview; b) necessary distinctions, basic terminology, a few statistics and foundational meanings; and, c) definitions for 3 Usages. In Chapter One- a) some reflections on a few preliminary illustrations; and, b) an identification of some key issues and tensions inherent in the concept of S/spirit. This helps the reader grasp the complexities and subtleties of the concept of S/spirit as it developed over time. Furthermore, it allows the reader to perceive and appreciate the ambiguity with which the concept of S/spirit developed and thus, hopefully, facilitates a degree of acceptance for and tolerance of competing models.

Necessary Distinctions, Basic Terminology, a Few Statistics, and Foundational Definitions.

Hebrew is the primary language of the Old Testament (OT). Greek is the primary language of the New Testament (NT). S/spirit is most often the English translation for the Hebrew ruach and/or the Greek pneuma.[2] H/holy is most often the English translation for the Hebrew qadosh and/or the Greek hagios. These are the primary terms of our investigation. Rarely in the OT does one find qadosh (holy) and ruach (spirit) together.[3] Yet, hagios (holy) and pneuma (spirit) are frequently joined in the NT.[4] This phenomenon is addressed at a later point in our study. But, for now, consider these additional statistics. Ruach occurs 378 times in the OT, whereas, pneuma occurs 379 times in the NT.[5] The near identical number might be considered coincidence or divine design, except for the fact that the OT is approximately 4x the length of the NT, making it apparent that the concept of S/spirit developed and received greater emphasis in the NT.[6] In light of the volume and frequency of these occurrences, the presentation here is necessarily selective and in accord with the needs and purposes of this study.

The most basic and root meaning of ruach/pneuma refers to the invisible but animating power of "air in movement, experienced as wind, breeze, or breath,"[7] known and sometimes appreciated for attending visible effects. These physical meanings are carried over, metaphorically, to refer to the invisible but animating power of God, whose effects can be seen and thus (hopefully) appreciated by the believing community. The invisibility and palpable power of the wind serve as a ready metaphor for the operations of an invisible and almighty God. This foundational understanding is suggested by the Psalmist. With regard to God, Psalm 104:4 declares: "who makest the winds (plural of ruach) thy messengers, flames of fire thy servants" (*NEB*). Psalm 104 is a celebration of God's activities in creation and is often understood as a reflection upon the creation account found in Genesis 1. The Psalmist treats the wind, or winds, as if they qualified as messengers for God. The notion of the speed with which the wind moves is suggested by subsequent Aramaic translations of Psalm 104.[8] Taken metaphorically, God's messengers (angels?) "are portrayed as executing the divine commands with the swiftness of wind and the strength of fire."[9]

These initial and foundational understandings of ruach/pneuma generate a rich but often ambiguous surplus of meanings for the concept of S/spirit. In large part, this is due to the "mysteriousness" so often associated with the workings of the wind and/or the animating power of God. My selection of some preliminary illustrations will portray the usage of S/spirit in a variety of contexts and functions. These contexts and functions run the gamut from various attributes and actions of God to various empowerments provided by God to human beings for the purposes of fulfilling His will. As a guide to our study, I now articulate three distinct usages of the term S/spirit. I also indicate their relative value from the perspective of the 4 Models. The difficulty we encounter in deciding upon a given usage consists in identifying contextual indicators (cues, clues, or criteria) by which we may more confidently decide for one usage over another.

3 Distinct Usages

Usage 1

Holy Spirit and/or Spirit functions as a synonym (alternate term of like meaning) or metonym (substitute term) for God. The transcendent and personal character or identity of God is emphasized in this usage. Specifically, God the Father is in view and thus, when this is determined to be the usage of a given occurrence, there is **no** room for any Trinitarian consideration. This usage finds favor among Unitarians. Trinitarians would allow for this usage in given contexts as long as it is acknowledged that there are other occurrences for which this usage does not suffice. The difficulty in determining this usage is that certain occurrences, in certain contexts, provide only weak contextual indicators of the stated emphases. Thus, in some cases, it is difficult to make a determination between Usage 1 and Usage 2 (described below). Often one is left to guess or to simply harmonize one's interpretation with one's commitment to a given model. Spirit would always be capitalized in this usage as it substitutes as a title or as a way of referring to a person.

Usage 2

holy spirit and/or spirit functions as a way of speaking about God's attributes, actions, or empowerments in relation to creation and/or His creatures. The immanent and impersonal aspects of God are in view in this usage. Since this usage would understand "spirit" as an "it," a presence, a power, an ability, or an influence the lower case "spirit" will always suffice. This usage finds favor with

Unitarians in that it eliminates the need for any reference to or hypothesis of a Third Person in the Godhead. Binitarians would understand this usage along similar lines as Unitarians. Trinitarians might allow for such a usage as long as some occurrences of Spirit would remain to justify their position. Part of the problem, however, is that Trinitarian translators and commentators often gloss over this possible usage, merging it with Usage 3 below. Again, the difficulty here is the same as the difficulty mentioned in Usage 1 above. In some cases, due to a lack of strong contextual indicators of the stated emphases, it is difficult to make a determination between Usage 1 and Usage 2.

Usage 3

Holy Spirit and/or Spirit functions as a way of referring to a distinct hypostasis in the Godhead other than God the Father and/or God the Son.[10] Capitalizing "Spirit" would be required in this Usage. Whether a given occurrence emphasizes the transcendent and personal identity of the reference or the immanent and impersonal aspects of the reference matters not. What matters is that this usage is best accounted for by the postulation of a Third Person (hypostasis) in the Godhead. This is specifically a Trinitarian usage and would be rejected by Unitarians and Binitarians. The difficulty in assigning this usage to a given occurrence is that it quite often results as an importation derived from the need to be consistent and faithful to those few, but deemed reliable, occurrences where a Trinitarian interpretation seems demanded. Hence, our study, of necessity, will carefully examine key Trinitarian texts (i.e., those texts which seem to present the Spirit as a 'person', as distinct from Father and Son, and as deity). Furthermore, this usage is complicated by the difficulties involved in distinguishing any given instance of "personification" from an instance of "hypostatization."[11]

(Note: The Non-Sectarian position recognizes that all three of the above usages can be argued for in a given occurrence. This position also maintains that it is precisely the inconsistency, ambiguity of usage, and difficulty of determining a given usage that justifies the Non-Sectarian position).

Notes

1. The concept of "person" is problematic, particularly when it comes to Trinitarian discussions. Helpful on the definitions and applications of the concept of "person" to Trinitarian thought is Donald Gelpi, *The Divine Mother: A Trinitarian Theology of the Holy Spirit* (Lanham: University Press of America, 1984), 103-125. Further comments on the notion of person will be provided in Chapter Three.

2. Hebrew and Greek words are transliterated according to the system provided by Edward Goodrick, *Do It Yourself Hebrew and Greek: Everybody's Guide to the Language Tools*. (Grand Rapids: Zondervan, 1976), 1:4 and 14:2.
3. 3x according to Horn, "Holy Spirit," in *The Anchor Bible Dictionary*, ed. David Noel Freedman, et. al. (New York: Doubleday, 1992), 261.
4. 92 x according to *ibid.*, 265.
5. *Ibid.*, 262 and 265.
6. My calculations are based on the pagination found in the *New English Bible with Apocrypha* [Oxford: 1970]. The OT with Apocrypha runs 1,440 pages. The NT runs 336 pages. 4 x 336=1,344, less than 100 pages of my 25% approximation.
7. Horn, "Holy Spirit," 261.
8. An Aramaic translation is referred to as a targum. Franz Delitzsch, *Commentary on the Epistle to the Hebrews, Volume1* (Minneapolis: Klock & Klock,1978, reprint of 1871 original), 74, provides this translation of one targum: "who maketh His messengers speedy as the wind, His ministers as strong as flaming fire."
9. F. F. Bruce, *The Epistle to the Hebrews: The New International Commentary on The New Testament* (Grand Rapids: Michigan, 1964), 18.
10. The Greek term "hypostasis" is commonly rendered as "person" in English. The term is problematic and will be discussed further in Chapter Three.
11. See Illustration Five, Personification and Hypostatization, page 72.

Chapter One
Preliminary Illustrations

Genesis 1:2

1:2: "And the earth was without form, and void; and darkness *was* upon the face of the deep. And the Spirit of God (ruach elohim) moved upon the face of the waters" (*KJV*).[1]

This is the first canonical occurrence of ruach. The context is the six-day creation account. The Hebrew text is "ruach elohim," translated as "the Spirit of God," or "God's Spirit," by the *ASV, AMP, BBE, CSV, DB, ESV, GNT, KJ21, MSG, NIV, NKJV, NLT, RSV, WB, WEB*, and the *YLT*, but "spirit of God" by *DR* and *JPS*, and "mighty wind" by *NAB* and *NEB*. Perhaps the author of Genesis is employing a double meaning here. One can easily imagine a "mighty wind" sweeping over the waters with potential mighty effects. One can also imagine that God, by the energy of his breath/spirit, is getting ready to do something. It's interesting to note that verse 3 states, "Then God said" (*KJV*). One breathes, then speaks. It is the energy of breath/spirit that enables one to communicate. Here in Genesis S/spirit and W/word work together to create the universe.

But which of our 3 Usages is most appropriate here? Obviously, the various translators I have cited disagree. Translating and capitalizing ruach as "Spirit," as indicated by the majority of versions, argues for Usages 1 or 3. Those versions employing the lower case "spirit" (*JPS* and *DR*) suggest Usage 2. Those versions translating ruach as "wind" (*NAB* and *NEB*) have moved on to usages outside the concern of our study.

Usage 3 seems ruled out, at least in terms of a meaning intended by the original author. The doctrine of the Trinity, at the time of the composition of Genesis (ca: 600-500 BCE), had not yet been heard of. Yet, many Trinitarian commentators specify this as the first occurrence of the Trinity.[2] Usage 2 commends itself in the sense that God is portrayed as immanent to creation via His "spirit." His spirit is "moving" (*DR, GNT*, and *KJV*), or "hovering" (*CSV, DB, ESV, JPS, NASB, NIV, NLT, RSV, and WEB*), or "sweeping" (*NEB*), or "brooding," (*AMP, MSG*), or "fluttering" (*YLT*) over the waters. The Hebrew word here is rachap.[3] God's patience, care, and creative power, are certainly the attributes in view. The orderly creation that follows appears to evolve out of the actions attributed to God in verse 2. It is not God in His personal identity that receives attention here, but God in His activity towards creation. Yet, one might try to make room for Usage 3 by calling attention to the enigmatic plural of Genesis 1:26: "Let Us make man in Our image. . .." (*KJV*). The "Us" might include: the Spirit of verse 2; the creative Word of verses 3-29; and the God (Elohim) spoken of throughout the account. This is an attempt to legitimate Usage 3 by moving from the immediate context to the remote context and at the same time giving consideration to later doctrinal developments.

A significant number of reputable scholars, however, interpret the "us" of Genesis 1:26 to refer to God and his angels.[4] Little heard, but contextually and substantially sound, is the suggestion that the "us" refers to the creative earth of Genesis 1:11, 12, and 24 and/or the creative waters of Genesis 1:20 and 21. Human beings are a mix of dirt, water, and spirit or consciousness.

Genesis 3:8

3:8: "And they heard the voice of the LORD God walking in the garden in the cool (ruach) of the day. . ." (*KJV*).

This is the second occurrence ruach.[5] The King James translators should be complimented here for such a rich and poetic translation. Obviously, ruach is simply used here to refer to the "cooling" effects of the wind (supporting the *KJV*'s "cool" are the *ASV, BBE, DB, JPS,* and *WB*; the *YLT* has "breeze.").This occurrence has little significance for the present study other than to illustrate ruach's primary associations with the wind.

Genesis 6:3

6: 3: "And, the Lord said, 'My spirit (ruach) shall not always strive with man, for that *he* also *is* flesh" (*KJV*).

This is the third canonical occurrence. The context is God's judgment upon the human race at the time of Noah's flood. By rendering ruach as lower case "spirit," several translators (*ASV; BBE; DR; JPS; KJV; NAB; RSV;* and *WB*.) suggest Usage 2. Those versions adopting a paraphrase translation style make this interpretation clearer. For example: "my life giving breath" (*CEV*); "my life giving spirit" (*NEB*); "I will not allow people to live forever" (*GNT*); and "I'm not going to breathe life into men and women endlessly" (*MSG*). Yet, several translations decided to capitalize Spirit (ruach) suggesting Usage 1 or 3 (*AMP; CSV; ESV; KJ21; NASB; NIV; NLT; NKJV; WEB;* and *YLT*).

A second key term in this passage is the *KJV*'s "strive" (Hebrew: diyn). Agreeing with the *KJV* are the *NASB, NKJV, WB, WEB,* and *YLT*. Other translations are: dwell (*AMP*); plead (*DB*); abide (*JPS* and *RSV*); contend (*NIV*); put up with (*NLT*); and remain (*CEV; CSV; DR; NAB*; and the *NEB*).

Given that translators differ, I will here attempt 3 interpretations satisfying the demands of each of my 3 Usages.

Usage 1: This would understand Spirit (ruach) as referring to God Himself, a synonym or metonym. The sense would be that God would not "put up with" (*NLT*) human rebellion forever and thus the flood appears justified.

Usage 2: This would understand spirit (ruach) as referring to God's "life-giving breath" (*CEV*). The sense would be that God would not continue to so gift human beings if their wickedness persisted.

Usage 3: This would understand Spirit (ruach) as referring to the Third Person of the Holy Trinity. In Trinitarian thought, distinctions are made regarding the "economic" functions of each member of the Godhead.[6] The Spirit functions as the one who positively sanctifies and/or negatively imposes temporal judgments upon the disobedient.

Genesis 41: 8

41:8: "And it came to pass in the morning that his spirit (ruach) was troubled; and he sent and called for all the magicians of Egypt, and all the wise men thereof: and Pharaoh told them his dreams; but *there was* none that could interpret *them* unto Pharaoh" (*KJV*).

I am skipping over several non-relevant occurrences of ruach in order to get to the next significant occurrence of ruach for this study.[7] In context, spirit functions as a synonym or metonym for Pharaoh. It is the need to call attention to the deeper or more hidden aspects of Pharaoh that seems to justify the use of the term "spirit." By reverse or inverse analogy, when "spirit" is used in relation to God, it is often for the purpose of calling attention to God's more visible or apparent operations. Ruach was not found capitalized in any of the versions I consulted. Some versions substituted "he" for "spirit" (*CSV; DR; GNT; MSG;* and *NLT*). The *NIV* used "mind" for ruach and the *CEV* simply put: "the king was so upset." This occurrence is helpful for the purposes of this study in that it presents an example where ruach is used interchangeably (as a synonym or metonym) for the person referred to. Unitarians are quick to point out that the relationship portrayed in this passage between "spirit" (ruach) and Pharoah provides an analogy for the many times that "spirit" is best viewed as simply interchangeable with "God." Since none of my 3 Usages apply in this example we move on to the next illustration.

Genesis 41: 38

4   Chapter One

41:38: "And Pharaoh said unto his servants, Can we find *such a one as* this *is*, a man in whom the Spirit of God *is*?" (*KJV*).

This is the next relevant occurrence of ruach. Also capitalizing "Spirit" are: the *CEV; DB; ESV; KJ21; NKJV; RSV*; and the *WEB*. Joseph's ability to interpret dreams provides the contextual evidence for Pharaoh's comment. But which Usage is justified here? Usage 1 might be justified on the basis of Joseph's statement in 41:25: "God hath shewed Pharaoh. . ." (*KJV*). The "Spirit of God," in 41:38, could be interpreted as a simple synonym for God's presence in Joseph. Usage 2 suggests that it is not God in His personal identity that is in view here, but rather God's gift of dream interpretation to Joseph. Usage 2, then, would down play the personal and transcendent aspects of God's being and demand a lower case "spirit" as is the case with the following versions: *ASV; AMP; BBE; CSV; DR; GNT; JPS; NAB; NIV; MSG; NLT;* and *YLT*. The *NASB* makes all this much clearer with the translation, "a divine spirit." Usage 3 could be justified anachronistically or dogmatically on the basis of the fact that references to the Spirit of God are references to the Third Person of the Trinity as justified by other biblical passages or upon the authority of Church councils.

I will now move from looking at relevant sequential occurrences of ruach to occurrences selected on the basis of their potential for illustrating both the diversity of meanings and the various tensions within the concept of S/spirit.

Exodus 28:3 and 31:3

28:3: "And thou shalt speak unto all *that are* wise hearted, whom I have filled with the spirit (ruach) of wisdom, that they may make Aaron's garments to consecrate him, that he may minister unto me in the priest's office" (*KJV*).
31:3: "And I have filled *him* with the spirit (ruach) of God, in wisdom, and in understanding, and in knowledge, and in all manner of workmanship" (*KJV*).

In context, these passages tell of God's empowerments to those who were selected to make special priestly garments and various furnishings for the holy tabernacle. These two Exodus passages seem to be speaking of the same reality, although one passage refers to this reality as "the spirit of wisdom" (28:3) and the other the "spirit of God" (31:3). Even the latter passage is qualified by "in wisdom, and in understanding, and in knowledge, and in all manner of workmanship." Thus, one might assume that in context the "spirit of God" is interchangeable with the "spirit of wisdom," or any of the other specified empowerments listed. All of the translations that I have been utilizing that employ the term "spirit" for ruach lower case "spirit" for "spirit of wisdom" in Exodus 28:3. However, many translations opt out of translating ruach as "spirit" in this instance, rendering the thought with a clearer paraphrase. For example: "I have endowed with skill and good judgment" (*AMP*); "only by persons who possess skills that I have given them" (*CEV*); "all the skilled workers to whom I have given ability" (*GNT*); and "to whom I have endowed with an able mind" (*RSV*). Consistent with this line of reasoning are the following translations which also lower case "spirit" when coming to the "spirit of God" in Exodus 31:3: *BBE; DB; DR; KJV;* and, *JPS*. The *GNT* puts "my power," and the *NAB* has "a divine spirit of skill."

Yet, the majority of translation committees balked at lower casing "Spirit of God" when coming to Exodus 31:3 (*ASV; AMP; CSB; ESV; KJ21; NASB; NIV; MSG; NLT; NKJV; RSV; WEB;* and *YLT*). What was going on here? Did these committees not discern the clear logic of the foregoing paragraph or the perceptive judgment of the other translators? Perhaps the reticence has to do with the larger issues of consistency. It seems that "ruach/Spirit" is translated as upper case when directly joined with the phrase "of God." Or, it could be based on a decision to be faithful to a Trinitarian understanding of the Spirit. Whatever the explanation, these passages were included as representative of many other cases where a contextual inconsistency can be spotted. I have just argued for Usage 2 for ruach in both Exodus 28:3 and 31:3, but the majority of translators appear to disagree by their decision to capitalize "ruach/Spirit" in 31:3.

Numbers 11: 16-17, and 25-31

11:16: "And the LORD said unto Moses, Gather unto me seventy men of the elders of Israel, *whom* thou knowest to be the elders of the people, and officers over them; and bring *them* unto the tabernacle of the congregation, that they may stand there with thee.

11:17: "And I will come down and talk with thee there: and I will take of the spirit (ruach[1]) which is upon thee, and will put *it* upon them; and they shall bear the burden of the people with thee, that thou bear *it* not thyself alone" (*KJV*).

11:25: "And the LORD came down in a cloud, and spake unto him, and took of the spirit (ruach[2]) that *was* upon him, and gave *it* unto the seventy elders: and it came to pass, *that*, when the spirit (ruach[3]) rested upon them, they prophesied, and did not cease.

11:26: "But there remained two *of the* men in the camp, the name of the one *was* El-dad, and the name of the other Me-dad: and the spirit (ruach[4]) rested upon them; and *they were* of them that were written, but went not out unto the tabernacle: and they prophesied in the camp.

11:27: "And there ran a young man, and told Moses, and said, El-dad and Me-dad do prophesy in the camp."

11:28: "And Joshua the son of Nun, the servant of Moses, *one* of his young men, answered and said, My lord Moses, forbid them."

11:29: "And Moses said unto him, Enviest *thou* for my sake? Would God that all the LORD's people were prophets, *and* that the LORD would put his spirit (ruach[5]) upon them!"

11:30: "And Moses gat him into the camp, *he* and the elders of Israel."

11:31: "And there went forth a wind (ruach[6]) from the LORD, and brought quails from the sea. . ." (*KJV*).

In this classic text, ruach occurs 6x. All the translations that I checked employed the word "S/spirit" (varying on upper and lower casing) for the first 5 occurrences. All employed the word "wind" for the 6th occurrence (verse 31) except for *YLT* going with "a spirit." There is little dispute regarding ruach as a reference to the physical force of the wind understood as the secondary agent by which "the LORD brought quails from the sea" in verse 31. What appears disputed is the usage of "S/spirit" in the first 5 occurrences. Should we understand these occurrences of ruach to refer to God as a person or as emphasizing his personal identity (Usage 1 or 3)? Or, does the context make it clear that ruach should be understood as referring to an impersonal empowerment, bestowed upon the recipient in varying portions and for varying durations (Usage 2)? It seems that those translators that decided to upper case "Spirit" have chosen the former (*AMP; ASV; CSV; DB; ESV; KJ21; MSG; NASB; NIV; NKJV; NLT; WEB;* and, *YLT*). It seems that those translators that decided to lower case "spirit" have chosen the latter (*BBE; DR; GNT; JPS; KJV; NAB;* and *RSV*). This typical 70-30% split illustrates the difficulty translators have when deciding upon an interpretation of ruach. At any rate, all these versions were consistent in either upper and/or lower casing ruach when translated as "S/spirit."

Usage 2 commends itself when one considers that the context has to do with Moses' need to "unburden" himself with the sole responsibility of leading the Israelites out of the desert and into the promise land. This is made clear from Numbers 11: 11-12:

11:11: "And Moses said unto the LORD, Wherefore hast thou afflicted thy servant? And wherefore have I not found favour in thy sight, that thou layest the burden of all this people upon me?"
11:12: Have I conceived all this people? Have I begotten them that thou shouldest say unto me, Carry them in thy bosom as a nursing father beareth the sucking child, unto the land which thou swarest unto their fathers?" (*KJV*).

Hence, verses 16-17 are to be understood as the LORD's response to Moses and verses 25-30 the actualization of that response. The "LORD" responded by promising to distribute to the seventy elders some of the spiritual leadership abilities that had been bestowed upon Moses. Chief among these abilities was the capacity for prophecy (verses 25-29). The *CEV* makes this clear by its decision to translate the first occurrence of ruach (verse 17) as: "I will give them some of your authority (ruach)." The matter of authority and using God-given talents to help Moses in his leadership responsibilities seems clear enough from the context. Therefore, Usage 2 seems most appropriate.

However, Usages 1 and/or 3 could be justified by the desire to emphasize that God is the source of this authority and retains ultimate control over its exercise and distribution. In addition, Usages 1 and/or 3 could be understood to encompass the notions of Usage 2 and thus would be understood to be a "more thorough" interpretation. Finally, Usages 1 and/or 3 may be understood as necessary for preserving the overall integrity of the scriptural teaching about the Spirit.

Psalm 51: 9-12

9: "Hide thy face from my sins, and blot out all mine iniquities,"
10: "Create in me a clean heart, O God: and renew a right spirit (koon ruach[1]) within me,"
11: "Cast me not away from thy presence; and take not thy holy spirit (qadosh ruach[2]) from me."
12: "Restore unto me the joy of thy salvation; and uphold me *with Thy* free spirit (nedibay ruach[3])" (*KJV*).

This is the most famous of the penitential psalms and has been associated by some interpreters with David's sin with Bathsheba, though this association is not demanded by the context, circumstance, or relevance of this psalm to the present investigation. There are 3 occurrences of ruach in this passage. In each occurrence ruach is modified by an adjective (right/holy/free). The parallelism of these lines tempts the interpreter to understand "right spirit," "holy spirit," and "free spirit" as variant ways of saying the same thing, or as a way of enlarging the thought of the first line by the subsequent two lines. Parallelism is the chief poetic device of all of Hebrew poetry and the three basic forms are synonymous parallelism, antithetic parallelism, and synthetic parallelism.[8] These considerations suggest Usage 2 for ruach in each of its 3 occurrences in Psalm 51: 9-12. It seems clear that the penitent of this psalm is praying for forgiveness and grace and a restoration of a right relationship with God. God's gifts are in view here rather than God in his personal identity or transcendence. By lower casing "spirit" in each of its 3 occurrences several versions appear to concur with this analysis (*BBE; DR; GNT; JPS; KJV; NAB;* and *NEB*).

Yet, again, we see a divergence from a consistent interpretation of ruach here in the majority of translators. Although all the versions I consulted lower case the first occurrence of "spirit," and almost all versions lower case the third occurrence (the *NKJV* is the exception translating the third occurrence of ruach as: "Your generous Spirit"), a great diversity appears when it comes to the second occurrence of ruach. Some capitalize both "Holy" and "Spirit" (*AMP; CEV; CSV; ESV; NASB; NIV; NLT; RSV;* and *YLT*), some capitalize just "Spirit," lower casing "holy," (*ASV; KJ21; NRSV; RSV* and *WEB*), and some also capitalize the preceding "Thy" or "Your" (*AMP; CSV; KJ21; NASB;* and *YLT*). What is going on here? It seems to me that either many translators have missed the poetic feature of parallelism mentioned above or they are concerned to uphold the overall teaching of scripture regarding the personality of the "Holy Spirit." It appears that a broader doctrinal concern has taken precedence over the demands of the immediate context. This latter consideration, it seems to me, is about all that one could appeal to for justifying Usage 1 and/or 3 in the case of Psalm 51: 9-12.

Before moving to my next illustration, allow me to share how the *MSG* paraphrases Psalm 51: 10-12:

51:10: "God, make a fresh start in me, shape a Genesis week from the chaos of my life."
51:11: "Don't throw me out with the trash or fail to breathe holiness in me."
51:12: "Bring me back from gray exile, put a fresh wind in my sails."

Although the translators of the *MSG* did not even utilize the word "S/spirit" in their translations of each occurrence of ruach, they certainly leave the reader with some vivid and contemporary idioms. I had never thought of praying "shape a Genesis week from the chaos of my life" but it certainly resonates with this student of the Bible. I occasionally have been grateful that my wife did not "throw me out with the trash" and can certainly feel its applicability to my walk with God. " Bring me back from gray exile" works well, in my opinion, as a substitute for "Restore unto me the joy of my salvation" (*KJV*), even though the only word similar in the translations is "me." And, "put a fresh wind in my sails" is certainly more idiomatic than "uphold me *with thy* free spirit" (*KJV*). This *MSG* paraphrase further argues for Usage 2.

Isaiah 11:1-2

11:1: "And there shall come forth a rod out of the stem of Jesse, and a Branch shall grow out of his roots."
11:2: "And the spirit (ruach[1]) of the LORD shall rest upon him, the spirit (ruach[2]) of wisdom and understanding, the spirit (ruach[3]) of counsel and might, the spirit (ruach[4]) of knowledge and of the fear of the LORD;" (*KJV*).

This classic text speaks of God's anointing on an ideal and future Davidic king. It is frequently read in conjunction with other "messianic" texts in Isaiah (7:14; 9:1-6; and 42:1). Christians see these passages fulfilled in the life and ministry of Jesus. Ruach occurs 4x in verse 2. The chief difficulty appears to revolve around whether the first occurrence is to be understood as equivalent to the subsequent occurrences. Does the first occurrence refer to God's gift of empowerment (in general) while the other three occurrences name specific empowerments? This would be our Usage 2. Or, Does the first occurrence refer to God Himself (the Father and/or the Third Person of the Trinity) while the other three occurrences refer to "gifts" of the Spirit? This would allow Usage 1 and/or 3 for the first occurrence and Usage 2 for the latter three. Translators, again, appear about evenly divided on this question. Here are the statistics.

Versions suggesting a consistent Usage 2 for all occurrences of ruach are: *BBE; DR; JPS; KJV; NAB;* and *WB*. Versions suggesting Usage 1 and/or 3 for the first occurrence but Usage 2 for the subsequent occurrences are: *ASV; DB; NASB; WEB*; and *YLT*. Some versions opted to consistently capitalize Spirit for all four occurrences of ruach, thus suggesting Usage 1 and/or 3 throughout (*AMP; NIV; NKJV;* and *NLT*).

How would one argue for the correct interpretation/translation? It would seem to me that an exhaustive study of the author's use of ruach throughout the text of Isaiah would be the first place to start. For our immediate and less involved purposes, the analysis just rendered helps illustrate, once again, the importance of a thorough and consistent policy for translating and interpreting the biblical concept of "S/spirit."

Isaiah 40:13 and I Corinthians 2: 16

Isaiah 40:13: "Who hath directed the Spirit (ruach) of the Lord, or *being* his counselor hath taught Him?" (*KJV*).

1 Corinthians 2: 16: "For who hath known the mind (nous) of the Lord, that he may instruct Him?" (*KJV*).

Isaiah is celebrating God's majesty and sovereignty in comparison with the might of other nations and their gods. In the NT, Paul echoes this passage in order to celebrate God's majesty and sovereignty with regard to the mystery of Christ (compare 1 Corinthians 2: 16 with 1 Corinthians 2: 7). Paul substitutes "mind/nous" (simple Greek word for mind) for Isaiah's "Spirit/ruach." Thus, for Paul, the ruach of Isaiah 40:13 is a reference to God "Himself." Translators might be making a grammatical judgment call in lower casing or upper casing the word "S/spirit." But the sense of the passage seems clear (at least to Paul). Ruach in Isaiah 40:13 and/or nous in 1 Corinthians 2:16 simply refer to the inner identity of the person being spoken of. How do the various versions handle these passages?

With regard to Isaiah 40:13, the following versions capitalized Spirit (*AMP; ASV; CSV; ESV; KJV; KJ21; NASB; NKJV; NLT; RSV; WB; WEB;* and *YLT*). The following versions lower cased spirit (*BBE; DR;* and *JPS*). Some versions bring out the sense of the passage by omitting the word S/spirit altogether. For example, the *CEV* states: "Has anyone told the Lord what he must do or given him advice?" The *GNT* states: "Can anyone tell the Lord what to do? Who can teach him or give him advice?" The *MSG* has: "Who could ever have told God what to do or taught him his business?" These paraphrases, in my judgment, make the thought of the passage clearer by omitting the word Spirit. This example seems peculiar in that, if the word S/spirit is retained, one could upper case or lower case "S/spirit," without misleading or confusing the reader. Clearly the reference is to God Himself, which best conforms to Usage 1.

But a probe into the context of 1 Corinthians 2 and the various renderings of the several occurrences of pneuma S/spirit there is revealing. Before citing the fuller context of 1 Corinthians 2, allow me to clear the air on how the various versions rendered nous/mind of 1 Corinthians 2:16. The following render "nous" as mind: *AMP; ASV; BBE; CSV; DBV; DR; ESV; GNT; KJV; KJ21; NAB; NASB; NIV; NKJV; NRSV; RSV; WB; WEB; WNT;* and *YLT*. The *CEV* and *NLT* have "thoughts." The *MSG* renders the Greek "nous" (mind) as Spirit. The *MSG* also makes the connection to Isaiah 40:13 explicit: "Isaiah's question, 'Is there anyone around who knows God's Spirit, anyone who knows what he is doing? has been answered: Christ knows, and we have Christ's Spirit."

I will now cite the fuller context of 1 Corinthians 2: 10-16 in order to make some other pertinent observations regarding the problem of translating/interpreting the word S/spirit (pneuma in Greek).

2:10: "But God hath revealed *them* unto us by his Spirit (pneuma^1); for the Spirit (pneuma^2) searcheth all things, yea, the deep things of God."
2:11: "For what man knoweth the things of a man, save the spirit (pneuma^3) of man which is in him? Even so the things of God knoweth no man, but the Spirit (pneuma^4) of God."
2:12: "Now we have received, not the spirit (pneuma^5) of the world, but the spirit (pneuma^6) which is of God; that we might know the things that are freely given to us of God."
2:13: "Which things also we speak, not in the words which man's wisdom teacheth, but which the Holy Ghost teacheth (pneuma^7); comparing spiritual things with spiritual."
2:14: "But the natural man receiveth not the things of the Spirit (pneuma^8) of God; for they are foolishness unto him; neither can he know *them*, because they are spiritually discerned" (*KJV*).

There are 8 occurrences of pneuma here, all translated as S/spirit or as "Holy Ghost" (occurrence 7). Occurrences 1, 2, 4, 7, and 8 are capitalized in the *KJV*. Occurrence 7 has added the word "Holy" (which has no corresponding term in the majority of critical Greek texts) and employed Ghost rather than Spirit. Surprisingly, there was greater conformity with this pattern among the various versions than I had expected. *KJ21* also had "Holy Ghost" for the 7th occurrence while many others included the unsubstantiated "Holy" though retaining the word "Spirit" for pneuma (*AMP; NKJV; WB; WEB; WNT;* and *YLT*). The *AMP* also included an unsubstantiated "Holy" before "Spirit" in occurrences 2 and 6. The most significant departure from the pattern established by the *KJV* was found in occurrence 6. The *KJV* has "spirit which is of God" (lower case) but all other versions except for *ASV* and *WB* rendered pneuma here as "Spirit" (upper case). One wonders what was in the mind of the translators. How did they understand the term pneuma in its several occurrences? More importantly, how did Paul understand his own successive usage of the term? Did he intend pneuma to refer to the same reality in each occurrence? Occurrences 3 and 5 can be left out of the difficulty here, as the former is a clear reference to the "spirit of man" and the latter is a clear reference to the "spirit of the world" (note: all versions lower case occurrences 3 and 5 unless omitting it altogether, as does the *NLT*, or employing another term, as does the *CEV*). If thus understood, why would translators oscillate between upper and lower casing the remaining occurrences (which all have a connection to God)? Why insert, as a few versions do, the unsubstantiated word "Holy" before the occurrences mentioned above? These are good questions and commentators are all over the map with answers. Before leaving these important considerations allow me to point out that Paul was comfortable substituting "nous/mind" in 1 Corinthians 2:16 for the "Spirit" of Isaiah 40:13. The reference clearly is to God Himself (Usage 1). Furthermore, the God-associated occurrences of pneuma in 1 Corinthians 2:10-14 (# 1, 2, 4, 6, 7, and 8) should also be understood along the same lines except that occurrence 6 seems to emphasize God's gift of a spiritual capacity for communion with His own Spirit and perhaps should be kept as lower case "spirit" in order to make that nuance apparent. This is one of several places where the distinction between Giver and gift, the Divine Spirit and the human spirit seems blurred and may suggest a mystical impulse.[9]

Isaiah 48:16

48:16: ". . .and now the LORD God and his Spirit (ruach) hath sent me" (*KJV*).

The reason for the inclusion of this illustration is that it may be the only OT verse that one could point to in order to suggest that the "Spirit" is another person alongside of God. It is not clear from the context whether the "me" of this passage refers to the prophet writing (Isaiah or Deutero-Isaiah) or to someone else (Cyrus?). This is really all beside the point for the purposes of our study. The critical question is how ruach is to be understood in this verse. Does ruach here refer to someone other than "the LORD God" but who also is God? Should "Spirit" be capitalized here? If not, how then should we understand "spirit" as the subject of "hath sent me"?

Translators are, again, all over the map. Two grammatical considerations are helpful prior to looking at the various versions. First, "hath sent me" (Hebrew: shaliach) is singular in form. This tempts some translators to question whether or not ruach is to be included in the subject of the verb. Second, the "and" of "and his Spirit" is the letter "vav" in Hebrew, referred to as "vav-consecutive" by Hebrew grammarians. This Hebrew conjunction encompasses a wide variety of possible meanings.[10] Hence, it is possible to render the Hebrew with the understanding that ruach (S/spirit) is the object rather than the subject of "hath sent. . ."

So what do the various versions do with this verse? The versions that interpret ruach as included within the subject of the verb are: *ASV; DB; KJV; KJ21; NASB; NKJV; NLT;* and *WB*. Those versions that treat ruach as the object of being sent are: *JPS; MSG; NAB;* and *RSV*. Several versions make attempts at smoothing out the difficulty with alternative renderings: "And now the Lord has sent His Spirit in and with me" (*AMP*); "the Lord God has sent me, and given me his spirit" (*BBE*); "by the power of his Spirit the LORD God has sent me" (*CEV*); and "Now the Sovereign Lord has given me his power and sent me" (*GNT*).

Admittedly, this is a difficult verse to translate. Whatever Usage one decides upon, it would seem reasonable to me to not give this verse much weight in supporting a given Model.

Isaiah 63: 9-11

63:9: "In all their affliction he was afflicted, and the Angel of His presence (malek paneh) saved them: in His love and in His pity he redeemed them; and he bare them, and carried them all the days of old."
63:10: "But they rebelled, and vexed His holy Spirit (qadosh ruach[1]): therefore He was turned to be their enemy and he fought against them."
63:11: "Then He remembered the days of old, Moses, and His people, *saying*, Where is He that brought them up out of the sea with the shepherd of his flock? where is He That put His holy Spirit (qadosh ruach[2]) within him?" (*KJV*).

In this passage the prophet reminds his listeners/readers in the 6th century BCE of God's past dealings with his people in the 13th century BCE. He seems to equate "the Angel of His presence" (63:9) with the "holy Spirit" of 63: 10 and 11. The past dealings in mind go back to Exodus 23: 20-23. These passages speak of the "angel" (malak/messenger) that God sent to lead the Israelites out of Egypt. A comparison with Exodus 33: 1-2 and 12-23 is instructive. In Exodus 33: 2, God again promises to send "an angel" (*KJV*) to help Moses lead his people. But later, in Exodus 33: 12, Moses complains to the LORD: "See, Thou sayest unto me, Bring up this People: and Thou hast not let me know whom Thou wilt send with me" (KJV). From the context, it appears that Moses is not happy with a mere "angel." He seems to want God Himself to accompany him. The remainder of the chapter seems to indicate that God responded and sent his "presence" (Exodus 33: 14; Hebrew: paneh/face) with Moses. So, Did God send his angel or did he go Himself? It seems that the biblical text is ambiguous, leaving one to wonder if the "angel of his presence" is equivalent to his "presence" and if these two phrases may also be interchangeable with "H/holy S/spirit" (qadosh ruach). Perhaps the biblical authors were not as concerned with the precise distinctions that modern interpreters, like myself and my readers, are concerned with. This is part of the argument of the Non-Sectarian Model.

Before sharing the results of the various English translations for Isaiah 63:9-11, let me point out that the interpretive significance of this possible conflation of "God's angel" with "his presence" and with "the H/holy S/spirit" will come back into play when we attempt to understand the background and function of the paraclete/comforter (referred to as the H/holy S/spirit) in the Gospel of John.[11]

Here is what the various versions do with qadosh ruach in Isaiah 63:10-11. The versions that upper case both Holy and Spirit are: *AMP; CEV; CSV; ESV; MSG; NASB; NIV; NKJV; NLT; NIV;* and *YLT*. Those that lower case holy but upper case Spirit are: *ASV; DB; KJV; KJ21; RSV; WB;* and *WEB*. Those that lower case both holy and spirit are: *BBE; GNT; JPS*; and *NAB*. So, Which Usage should apply here? It seems to me that Usage 2 would make the most sense given the context, especially the suggested interchangeability of "angel" with "presence" and with "holy spirit." The fact that the "holy spirit" was "rebelled" against and "vexed" does not demand that the "holy spirit" here is a person, much less a distinct person within the Godhead (Usage 1 or 3). A minimalist interpretation would see the "gift" of God's presence, and all that that might entail (the fruit of the spirit: love; joy; peace; etc; various manifestations of the spirit: prophecy; words of knowledge and wisdom; gifts of healing; etc.) as being "personified" here. A maximalist interpretation would seek to eliminate the (unnecessary?) figure of speech (personification) and make it clear, by being literal, that God Himself was the One rebelled against and vexed. Deciding between these alternatives is a "vexing" problem for those that adhere to one or the other of the first three Models.

Ezekiel 36:26-27

36:26: "A new heart also will I give you, and a new spirit (ruach^1) will I put within you: and I will take away the stony heart out of your flesh, and I will give you an heart of flesh."
36:27: "And I will put my spirit (ruach^2) within you, and cause you to walk in my statutes, and ye shall keep my judgment, and do *them*" (KJV).

Ezekiel prophesies of a restoration for the people of Israel after their return from exile in Babylon. This prophecy is one of many concerning an outpouring of God's S/spirit in the last days.[12] A poetic parallelism is suggested by these two verses and for our purposes the critical issue is deciding between synonymous parallelism or a graduated parallelism. In other words, does "new spirit" equal "my spirit"? Or, Does "my spirit" represent an advance in meaning and thought upon "new spirit"? Put even another way: Does "new spirit" of verse 26 refer to the "renewed" spirit of human beings, which interchangeably could be referred to as the "my spirit" of verse 27? Or, Does the "my spirit" of verse 27 represent a substantive addition in thought to what was expressed in verse 26? Again, from the perspective of the Non-Sectarian Model, I point out that Ezekiel and his earlier interpreters (Joel; Peter; Paul) may have not "looked for" or "considered" such a distinction.

So what is suggested from a perusal of the various versions? All versions that translate the ruach of verse 26 as "spirit" do so with a lower case. But it's regarding the ruach of verse 27 that translators differ. Upper casing ruach as "Spirit" are: *AMP; ASV; CEV; CSV; DB; ESV; KJ21; MSG; NASB; NIV; NKJV; NLT; WEB;* and *YLT*. Lower casing "spirit" are: *BBE; DR; GNT; JPS; KJV; NAB; NEB; RSV;* and *WB*. We have close to that typical 70-30 split I mentioned earlier. My comments at the end of the analysis above on Isaiah 63: 10-11, regarding minimalist and maximalist approaches seems relevant here.

Key Issues and Tensions

This introduction has raised several key issues and has identified several tensions within the concept of S/spirit. Among key issues are: the 3 Usages and the 4 Models; identifying clear criteria for determining one Usage over another; determining whether or not it is clear that these criteria are present in a given passage; translation policies on upper and lower casing S/spirit; and the difficulty of separating the person of the Giver (Spirit) from his gift(s) (spirit and corresponding endowments). I will address each of these briefly and then move on to some tensions that I have highlighted as well as some tensions that are yet to be made evident.

One might say that my 3 Usages have been arbitrarily constructed. Perhaps. Bible interpreters, theologians, and translation committees may choose to define "Holy Spirit" and/or "holy spirit" some other way and, of course, are free to do so. But the 3 Usages that have been constructed for the purposes of this study have been constructed in light of 4 competing Models. In that sense, I trust that they are not arbitrary. Each of the 4 Models finds support from a variety of Jewish and/or Christian denominations. The Unitarians find support from Jewish (and Islamic interpreters) as they concur on the notion that God is one, both in person and in essence. Among denominations that would support a Unitarian position are: Unitarian Universalist; Unity; Jehovah's Witnesses; Oneness Pentecostal; The Way International; Association for Christian Development; Seventh Day Church of God; Christadelphians; Christian Science; some derivatives of the Worldwide Church of God; and many non-denominational churches. Binitarianism appears to have appeal with various independent scholars, a few independent churches, and is claimed by its adherents as the predominant view of the early Christians prior to the 4th century. Trinitarianism, the majority position, is supported by Roman Catholics, Eastern Orthodox, and all major Protestant denominations. The issue of "arbitrariness" quickly becomes united with the issue of authority. Since all these denominations have the right, and therefore authority within their own traditions, to interpret H/holy S/spirit as they see fit, then the various Bible interpreters, theologians, and translation committees associated with a given tradition are often constrained by the authority of their respective traditions. My brief analysis of how S/spirit has been interpreted in a few selected texts illustrates that, especially in light of the divergence of translations among the versions, "faith" may be getting in the way of "reason," if in fact any reason is to be found. The irony of the divergent translations/interpretations of "S/spirit" is that it is to this "S/spirit" that the various interpreters appeal for guidance and claim as the basis for the authority and legitimacy of their interpretive decisions.

What about criteria? In the passages we have investigated, I have attempted to decide for a given Usage (1, 2, or 3) by appealing to contextual cues or clues. Cues or clues are simply those features of a passage that cohere with the stated definition or emphasis of a given Usage. In general, Usage 1 emphasizes the personal and transcendent aspects of God. It answers in the affirmative these questions: Is the ruach or pneuma (S/spirit) mentioned best understood as referring to an identifiable, self-aware, and volitional person (i.e., God the Father and/or God the Spirit)? Is "person" the first and foremost category that comes to mind from a plain reading of the text and context? Does the category of "person" withstand sustained reflection upon the occurrence in context? Specifically, Usage 1 has commended itself when the Spirit was seen as the subject of a verb ("moved," Genesis 1:2; "strive," Genesis 6:3; "knowing," 1 Corinthians 2:11; "teaching," 1 Corinthians 2:13; and "sending," Isaiah 48:16) or even as the object of a verb ("directing," Isaiah 40:13; "rebelling against," and "vexing," Isaiah 63: 10).

Usage 2 emphasizes the impersonal and immanent aspects of God's attributes, actions, or empowerments. In general, it answers these questions: Is the ruach/pneuma (S/spirit) mentioned best understood as referring to a "thing," an "it," an ability, power, or enablement of some kind? Is "impersonal gift" the first and foremost category that comes to mind from a plain reading of the text and context? Does the category of an "it" withstand sustained reflection? Specifically, Usage 2 has commended itself when "spirit" was viewed as the medium or power through which something was accomplished ("moving the waters," Genesis 1:2; "enlivening human beings," Genesis 6:3; "interpreting dreams," Genesis 41:8; "uttering prophetic words," Numbers 11:26; "sensing that all is right," Psalm 51: 9-12; "acting with wisdom, understanding, counsel, and might," Isaiah 11:2; "knowing the things of God," 1 Corinthians 2:12; and, "walking in the statutes and judgments of God," Ezekiel 36: 26-27).

In general, Usage 3 emphasizes all that Usage 1 does but with the added notion that the Spirit is a hypostasis or person in the Godhead distinct from Father and Son. Thus far, we have looked only at one text that "seems" to portray the Spirit as distinct from the Father and also as deity (Isaiah 48:16). But, due to grammatical difficulties, this usage was not entirely clear.

Speaking of grammatical difficulties. The major difficulty in this study, thus far, has been the vexing problem of capitalization. In general, style manuals agree that the name of a person understood to be deity is to be capitalized. Manuals differ on conventions regarding related pronouns and adjectives (perhaps explaining why there is a great deal of variation on upper or lower casing H/holy when proceeding S/spirit). The various versions we have looked at thus far are far from agreement among each other on the upper and lower casing of S/spirit and at times appear confused and inconsistent even within their own versions.

This brief review of our preliminary illustrations brings into focus the next issue: How easy is it to separate Giver (Spirit) from gift (spirit)? From a pastoral perspective, I would say that any gift that God (the Giver) gives is ultimately intended for the recipient and the benefactors to better "know, love, and serve" (quoted from memory from my 2nd grade *Baltimore Catechism*) the God who so richly blesses in such a variety of ways. Most often, when I give gifts, I want the recipient to enjoy the "thing" that I have given, but I also give in order to enhance my personal relationship with the recipient. But does this pastoral insight justify a dismissal of the dispute among adherents of the 4 Models? Which adherent of which Model should we ask? The interpretive problem remains. Thus, my reflections continue: a) to enhance ecumenism; and, b) to continue to pursue "the truth." A (hopefully helpful) chart illustrating how each of the various Models might picture the relationships between Giver and gift is provided on pages 69-71.

Finally, let me identify some of the tensions inherent in the concept of S/spirit, some we have encountered and some are yet to come. The Spirit may be viewed as personal agent (e.g., Isaiah 40:13) or as impersonal power (Exodus 28:3 and 31:3). Whether they can and should be separated is a matter of dispute among adherents of the 4 Models. The S/spirit has a corporate (e.g., Numbers 11:17), but also an individual dimension (e.g., Psalm 51: 9-12). Another tension that has and will emerge again is in regard to the relation of the Spirit to God the Father (e.g., Isaiah 48:16) and God the Son. Is the Spirit equal or subordinate? If subordinate, is the subordination one of essence or rank? Another important tension that could be explored is that between demand (e.g., Ezekiel 36: 27b "and cause you to walk in my statutes") and gift (e.g., Ezekiel 36:27 "And I will put my spirit within you"). The S/spirit, whether understood as a person or as a "thing," certainly is a gift and brings a variety of gifts. But as with any gift, there comes an obligation, or a demand to utilize the gift for its intended end. This brings us to the next tension. Is possession of the S/spirit temporary or permanent? Certainly an abuse of the gift of S/spirit might require its retraction. Some would quickly add here the tension between seeing the S/spirit as "with" us versus "in" us. Is the gift of S/spirit complete or partial? If partial, how does one understand the S/spirit as a person? How can a person be apportioned?

Several other tensions come to mind. We have seen the S/spirit indicated by external signs (e.g., Numbers 11:25-31) and through interior transformation (Psalm 51:9-12). The S/spirit is often presented as something "present" but also "future." The S/spirit may be seen at work in regeneration or in revelation, in justification or in sanctification. The S/spirit has a particular relationship with the Father, but also with the Son. And, finally, but not exhaustively, I conclude with the tension of a pre-Christ event understanding of the S/spirit versus a post-Christ event understanding of the S/spirit. This latter tension, in my judgment, is critical when deciding which of the 4 Models comes closest to the "truth." The reader thus is alerted to this critical tension and can anticipate an exposition of it in one or the other of the various expositions of the 4 Models to which we now turn.

Notes

1. Here and throughout, *italics* are original to *KJV*. The insertion of Hebrew/Greek words are my additions.
2. R. P. C. Hanson, *The Search for the Christian Doctrine of God* (Edinburgh. T & T Clark, 1988), 327, lists among the 27 anathemas of the First Sirmian Creed in 351 CE the statement: "If anyone says that at Gen 1:26, 'Let us make man', God was talking to himself [and not to the Son]." This makes it apparent that earlier than 351 CE Trinitarian theologians were in agreement on how to interpret Genesis 1:26. Douglas McCready, *He Came Down from Heaven: The Pre-existence of Christ and the Christian Faith* (Downers Grove: Intervarsity Press), 224, notes: "early commentators believed the plural 'we' to refer to the Trinity."
3. Francis Brown, S. R. Driver, and Charles A. Briggs, *A Hebrew and English Lexicon of the Old Testament*, rev. ed. (Oxford: Clarendon, 1972), define rachap as "*move gently*, also *cherish* and *brood*," 934 (italics original).
4. Gerhard VonRad, *Genesis* (Philadelphia: Westminster, 1961), is typical. He states: "The extraordinary plural...prevents one from referring God's image too directly to God the Lord. God includes himself among the heavenly beings and thereby conceals himself in this multiplicity" 58.
5. My source for the sequence of occurrences is: *The Englishman's Hebrew and Chaldee Concordance* (Grand Rapids: Zondervan, 1970), 1160-62.
6. See Killian McDonnell, *The Other Hand of God: The Holy Spirit as the Universal Touch and Goal* (Minnesota: Liturgical Press Collegeville, 2003), 213-29.
7. Genesis 6:17; 7:15, 22; 8:1; and 26:25.
8. See E. W. Bullinger, *Figures of Speech Used in the Bible* (Grand Rapids: Baker. 1968; reprint of 1898 original), 349-62.
9. See Evelyn Underhill, *Mysticism: The Nature and Development of Spiritual Consciousness* (Oxford: OneWorld, 2004, reprint of 1910 original), 109-24.
10. See Francis Brown, S. R. Driver, and Charles A. Briggs, A *Hebrew and English Lexicon of the Old Testament, rev.ed.* (Oxford: Clarendon 1972), 251-55.
11. See Chapter Three, pages 44-48.
12. Joel 3:1-3 and Isaiah 44:3 are understood by Christians as fulfilled at Pentecost and in the early Christian movement according to Acts 2:17-21.

Chapter Two
The Unitarian Model

My presentation of the Unitarian model is in three parts. First, I set forth a brief summary of the Unitarian position. Second, I expand upon several of the arguments found in the Unitarian position. And, third, I provide an exegesis of selected "H/holy S/spirit" passages that are relevant to the Unitarian position.

Brief Summary of the Unitarian Position

The first and central point of the Unitarian position is the recognition of the Bible's clear and unambiguous declaration that there is one God. Quite often this one God is explicitly identified as the Father. Scriptures declaring either the Son (Jesus) or the spirit to be God are not clear but susceptible of explanations which bring them into harmony with the passages which assert that God is one, frequently and metaphorically referred to as the (our) Father.

The Bible is clear regarding both the non-deity of Jesus and his distinction from the One God who is the Father. Jesus on more than one occasion denies that he possesses the prerogatives of deity (eternality, omnipotence, omniscience) and clearly proclaims that God is one and other than himself. Jesus is clearly presented as dependent to and subordinate to his God and his Father both in his earthly ministry and in his resurrected state. Passages that seem to "equate" Jesus with God are best understood in a functional rather than in an ontological sense. Jesus is better understood as God's agent of revelation and salvation in terms of an exalted human being or an exalted and pre-existent angelic being.

Furthermore, the spirit is never presented as the recipient of prayer or worship in either the OT or the NT. Rather, the model of worship appears to be that God (the Father) is worshipped through the agency of the Son in the power of the spirit. The affirmations of the previous two sentences are reinforced when one notes that there is an absence of any polemic in the NT regarding the status of the spirit as a deity. Debates regarding the status ascribed to Jesus abound, but the NT is silent regarding any conflict over the status of the spirit. This seems odd if the early church really had received a new revelation regarding the status of the spirit. It seems safer to assume that early Christians understood the spirit within the constraints of first century Jewish monotheism.

Unitarians acknowledge that the NT frequently presents God, Jesus, and the spirit together as a triad or in a triadic formula, but these presentations are not explicit regarding a Tri-unity of persons, and thus Unitarians look for alternative and plausible explanations that contribute to a more parsimonious reading of scripture.

One serious and problematic issue in the debate over the status of the spirit has to do with passages which "seem" to present the spirit as a person and as distinct from the Father and/or Son. Unitarians are quick, however, to point out that the majority of occurrences of spirit portray the spirit as an "it," employing impersonal categories or metaphors of an impersonal nature. Quite often the S/spirit is presented as a substance that can be poured out or applied in varying quantities, not something easily reconciled with the notion of a person. Those few but persistent passages which "seem" to present the spirit as a person are better understood as personifications, literary over determinations, or reifications of the means of revelation.

Unitarians find support in their view by appealing to source, form, and editorial considerations in the exegesis of relevant NT texts. Some examples will be provided below. The key component of their argument with regard to these texts is that the earlier layers of the developing Christian tradition present an understanding of the spirit more in line with previous Jewish understandings of the spirit.[1] The later developments, properly understood, do not point in a Trinitarian direction but have been so misunderstood by later Trinitarian interpreters.

Finally, Unitarians closely examine the ongoing debates about the relationships of God to Christ and spirit in the second to fourth centuries. They conclude that Christian apologists and theologians slowly but surely strayed from Judaism's clear monotheistic base, ending with the misguided affirmation of the Trinity. The lack of clarity and consistency of Trinitarian language and formulas among theologians from the second to the fourth century lends support to their view. Heresy seems unavoidable to any theologian committed to articulate the doctrine of the Trinity with any precision.[2] In the end, Unitarians conclude, one's affirmation of the Trinity rests upon acceptance of Church authority rather than upon a responsible and critical exegesis of scripture. The doctrine of the Trinity appears as a mystification of scripture and tradition rather than its clarification.

An Expansion of the Above Arguments

The unambiguous declaration that there is one God, the Father

Unitarians maintain that the metaphor "father" is applied to God in a sense that is simple, comprehensible, consistent, and defensible against the backdrop of the scriptures. God is "father" to all in the sense that he is the origin of all creation and in the sense that he exercises paternal care and nurture. God could also be conceived as "mother," although the scriptures do not emphasize this conception as much as the other, largely, in my judgment, due to the patriarchy of the times. God as "father," in traditional patriarchy, emphasizes God's authority, might, prerogatives, discipline, and beneficence. God as "mother" tends to emphasize affection, nurture, intimacy, and care. These two metaphors, taken together, provide a balance to transcendent and immanent notions of God. Thus, Unitarians often invoke God as "Father-Mother" or "Mother-Father."

The Trinitarian conception of God as "father" labors under the difficulties of having to clarify or having to ignore the precise sense in which God is presented as "father" in a given passage. In Trinitarian understanding, God is uniquely Father to the Son in the sense that he begets the Son from all eternity.[3] The Spirit is not begotten but proceeds from the Father, and so in relation to the Spirit the Father is not "father" but "spirator." God is also "father" to Jesus in his human nature, understood in the context of the virginal conception of Jesus by Mary.[4] But confusion enters when the one God, understood as Father-Son-Spirit, is also understood as "father" to all. In any given reference, when God is portrayed as "father," Trinitarians are confounded by the problem of these distinctions. For Unitarians the matter is simplified, as the following examples illustrate.

Ephesians 4:4-6

Paul exhorts the Ephesians to endeavor "to maintain the unity of the S/spirit in the bond of peace."[5] I waffled on the capitalization of S/spirit in order to engage the reader in an additional interpretive problem. Paul reinforces his exhortation to unity by calling his reader's attention to a series of singular realities that they all share in (one body, S/spirit, hope, Lord, faith, baptism, God and Father; 4:4-6). Is this one God the father in the sense that: (a) he is distinct from the Son and Spirit; and/or (b) as superior in rank, but not in essence, to the Son and the Spirit, he receives special reference when the one "God" is mentioned? Or, (c) is this one God the "father" in the sense that, as the one God (Father-Son-Spirit), he functions as the source and provider of all?

Unitarians sidestep this muddle. There is one God who is father, the source and provider of all. God the Father does not share his godhead with anyone.[6] The Son represents the Father and God's gift of spirit makes that representation real and effective. Jesus is distinguished from the one God the Father here, not as "Son" but as "Lord" of the Church. Paul makes it clear that this one God is "the God and Father of our Lord Jesus Christ" (1:3; *KJV*). The triadic, or Trinitarian, "hint" in this passage (one Lord, one S/spirit, one God [Father]) stands or falls upon one's decision regarding S/spirit. In context, Unitarians argue, it is clear that "spirit" (pneuma in Greek) should be lower case as Paul is emphasizing the "manner" or "mode of conduct" in which believers live and cooperate with one another in their various ministries within the body of Christ (see especially verses 11-32). It is interesting that only 2 of my 25 versions agreed with this point, and only 1 version fully. The *NAB* was the only version to lower case spirit (pneuma) in Ephesians 4:3 but inconsistently, in my judgment, upper cased Spirit (pneuma) in verse 4. The *MSG* offered this interesting (and consistent!) paraphrase: "(verse 3) alert at noting differences and quick at mending fences. (verse 4) You were called to travel on the same road and in the same direction, so stay together, both outwardly and inwardly." Compare the above with the traditional *KJV*: (verse 3) "Endeavouring to keep the unity of the Spirit in the bond of peace. (verse 4) *there is* one body, and one Spirit, even as ye are called in hope of your calling."

John 17:1-5

Another example demonstrating the attractive simplicity of Unitarian interpretation is found in John 17:1-5. Jesus is presented as praying to his Father (verses 1 and 5) just prior to his arrest, trial, and crucifixion. In verse 3, Jesus states: "And, this is life eternal, that they might know thee the only true God, and Jesus Christ, whom thou hast sent" (*KJV*). In context, Jesus addresses God as Father and as the "only true God." Believers, then, are to understand that this Father, revealed through Jesus Christ, is the "only true God." But is God's "fatherhood" to be understood in its special Trinitarian sense, namely as "Father" distinguished from "Son" and/or "Spirit"? The context does seem to support this distinction as Jesus presents himself in this prayer as the Father's 'pre-existent' Son (verses 1 and 5). So, it would seem, if Trinitarians take their terms from scripture and use them consistently. But, then, how can the Father, in this sense, be the "only true God"? In Trinitarian theology, the only true God is "Father, Son, and Holy Spirit." It would seem that Trinitarians must waffle in their understanding on either "father," or on "only true God," as one cannot have it both ways without contradiction.[7] Unitarians solve the dilemma by understanding God to be one person, the father. Jesus is either an exalted human being or the first created among God's creations (his Firstborn, Word, Son, etc.). There is only one true God, the Father.

I Corinthians 8:6

This last assertion is made plain in Paul's statement in 1 Corinthians 8:6: "But to us *there is but* one God, the Father, of whom are all things, and we in him; and one Lord Jesus Christ, by whom *are* all things, and we by him" (*KJV*). In context, Paul is dealing with the problem of eating meat offered to idols (verses 1-13). He recognizes that, although an idol in itself is nothing (verse 4), gentiles believe that these idols represent or are related to the worship of various "gods" and "lords" (verse 5). He then contrasts gentile belief with Christian belief regarding "gods" and "lords" (verse 6). The critical issue is not the apparent declaration that there is one God (both in verses 4 and 6), and that this one God is father (verse 8), but how Paul understands the distinction between 'gods" and "lords" (verse 5) and how he applies that distinction when assigning the term "god" to the father, and the term "lord" to Jesus. In other words, in Paul's use of the terms "gods/god" and "lords/lord," is there justification for a clear difference between these terms? Or, does Paul use these terms synonymously and with equivalent weight?

A further complication in the exegesis of this passage is whether or not Paul is consciously echoing Deuteronomy 6:4: "Hear, O Israel: The Lord *our* God *is* one Lord" (*KJV*). If so, as many argue, Paul is "splitting" the standard Jewish formula and affirmation of monotheism between God the Father, and Jesus the Lord, affirming that the one God includes both persons. If this exegesis is sound, and it is hotly debated, it, at the explicit level, supports binitarianism rather than trinitiarianism.[8] Why is it that the Holy Spirit always gets left out? Unitarians are happy to sidestep the debate over whether this passage echoes Deuteronomy 6:4 and rest confident in its plain meaning (that there is one God, the father) until they can be convinced otherwise or until the scholarly consensus is just so overwhelming that it would be unreasonable to resist it. But, this still leaves their position on possible distinctions between "god/s" and "lord/s" unaddressed.

The designation "god" functions as a title attributed to a deity in regard to status as an immortal entity worthy of respect or reverence, whereas, the designation "lord" refers to the exercise of authority over servants or subjects.[9] The terms are somewhat correlative. All gods are lords as they exercise authority over their subjects in their respective spheres of dominion. But, not all lords are gods, as many lords are simply lesser deities, angels, or human beings who are granted the prerogative of the exercise of authority within the sphere and domain of another. For examples: kings have lordship; husbands have lordship; and, owners of slaves have lordship but not the status of god—unless they are seen as significantly embodying the god's authority and thus represent the god and thus can be called god.[10]

So how does this summary of the meanings and connotations and distinctions between god and lord apply here in 1 Corinthians 8:6 and inform one in the debate over Unitarianism and Trinitarianism? Well, the alleged inclusion of Jesus into the Godhead, Unitarians argue, is not clear. What is clear, from other NT passages, is that Jesus' lordship (exercise of authority) is one that is given to him by God. According to Acts 2:36, God [the Father] "has made him [Jesus] both Lord and Messiah" (*NAB*). According to 1 Corinthians 11:3, God [the Father] is "the head of Christ" (*NAB*).[11] Thus, taking kephale in its metaphorical sense, God the Father is the "Lord" of the exalted Christ. According to Philippians 2: 6-11, Jesus' lordship is a gift from God and is better understood in a functional rather than in an ontological sense.[12] Philippians 2:9 states: "Wherefore also God him [Jesus] has lifted up and graced him with the name above all names" (my paraphrase).[13] According to 1 Corinthians 15:24-28, Jesus' exercise of lordship will one day terminate. Verse 28 reads: "When everything is subjected to him, then the Son himself will also be subjected to the one who subjected everything to him, so that God may be all in all" (*NAB*). Collectively, all these verses add up to saying that the lordship of Jesus is derivative, temporary, and subordinate in relation to the true God. Bietenhard states: "Primitive Christianity saw no infringement of monotheism in the installation of Jesus as Lord, but rather its confirmation."[14] These clear passages are deemed helpful in Unitarian attempts to harmonize what appears to be clearly taught in several passages with what is problematic in other passages, such as 1 Corinthians 8:6.

Apparent affirmations of the deity of the Son

Do any passages in the NT explicitly affirm the deity of Jesus, the notion that Jesus is equal in essence to God the Father? Unitarians say, no. Binitarians and Trinitarians say, yes. Non-Sectarians insist that the evidence is ambiguous. So what is the evidence? Since tomes have been written on this topic, my treatment will be selective but hopefully sufficient to indicate the Unitarian position. My approach is two-fold. First, I comment on passages that appear to deny that Jesus is God. Second, I comment on passages that attribute the title "God" to Jesus.

In addition to the logic developed above, with regard to the clarity of NT teaching concerning the Father as the only true God, I now add comment to select passages that deny the attribution of deity to Jesus outright.

Mark 10:18

Consider Mark 10:18: "And Jesus said unto him, why callest thou me good? *there is* none good but one, *that is*, God" (*KJV*). Jesus is responding to an inquisitor who, in his questioning, addressed Jesus as "Good Master" (Mark 10:17; *KJV*). This passage is puzzling. What was the inquisitor's intention? Was it flattery? Was it worship? Was it a genuine compliment? And, what about Jesus' response? Was it rejection of flattery? Was it rejection of worship? Of the commentaries that I consulted, Malina and Rohrbaugh (1992) were most helpful. They state:

> In a limited good society, compliments indicate aggression; they implicitly accuse a person of rising above the rest of one's fellows at their expense. Compliments conceal envy, not unlike the evil eye. Jesus must fend off the aggressive accusation by denying any special quality of the sort that might give offense to others. Such a procedure is fully in line with the canons of honor.[15]

Hence, Jesus wards off the challenge of the inquisitor with his counter question and the envy with his proverbial reference to the one God. This interpretation preserves the plain sense of the passage. Jesus denies that he is God.

Mark 13:32

Also in Mark's gospel, Jesus denies being omniscient, an attribute essential to deity. In the context of predictions about his second coming, Jesus states: "But of that day and *that* hour knoweth no man, no, not the angels which are in heaven, neither the Son, but the Father" (Mark 13:32; *KJV*). Trinitarians often invoke here the distinction between Jesus' human nature and his divine nature, attributing the ignorance to Jesus' human nature. But the importation of this distinction violates the clear and intended meaning of the author as intended for his original audience. All reading Mark's gospel at the time of its composition would conclude that since Jesus is not omniscient he is not God. Trinitarians admit that the doctrine of two natures and two wills in the person of Christ took time to develop (culminating in the confession of Chalcedon in 451 CE) but fail to provide a satisfactory exegesis of this plain passage.

John 6:38

Speaking of two natures and two wills in the person of Christ, consider this passage from John 6:38. Jesus states, "For I came down from heaven not to do mine own will, but the will of him that sent me" (*KJV*). To which will does Jesus refer in this passage, his divine will, his human will, or both? There are three locations in this passage where a will is expressed: 6:38a expresses the decision to come down from heaven; 6:38b expresses the doing of his own will, presumably on earth; and 6:38c expresses the will of the one who sent Jesus. 6:38a cannot literally refer to Jesus' human will, as it seems to refer to an action prior to his becoming human. 38b must refer to Jesus' human will, as it is the only will that could be distinguished from the divine will. 38c is clearly a reference to the divine will. But 38a and 38b only make sense as the expression of the separate will of a separate individual. Unitarian interpretation allows for two plausible explanations. One, Jesus is a pre-existent created spirit being who is one in person, nature, and will. His decisions to come down from heaven and to not do his own will while on earth appear congruous. Two, the phrase "came down from heaven" is not to be taken literally, as if Jesus literally pre-existed. Rather, it is a figurative way of referring to God the Father's foreknowledge and plan of salvation. Jesus' "pre-existence" is ideal rather than real.[16] Jesus is speaking here ideally, affirming his desire to do what God had pre-determined him to do. The Trinitarian view crumbles under its own weight, unable to offer a satisfactory resolution of the "wills" expressed in 38a and 38b.

John 16:13

This is an opportune moment to slightly digress but in a very relevant direction. A similar problem exists in John's gospel with regard to the will of the

Paraclete, the promised H/holy S/spirit of John 14-16. John 16:13 declares: "Howbeit when he, the Spirit of Truth, is come, he will guide you into all the truth; *for he shall not speak of himself*; but whatsoever he shall hear, that shall he speak" (*KJV*). I took liberties to *italicize* the critical phrase. If, as most Trinitarians argue, the Spirit of Truth=the Holy Spirit=The Third Person of the Trinity, then what sense is one to make of this passage? Does the Holy Spirit have two wills? Is one will interdependent with the Father and Son and the other separate from them? Perhaps I should refrain from what appears arcane. Does the Holy Spirit take vacations from the Father and the Son? If one wishes to press Trinitarians to own up to the implications of their teaching, then the following question seems pertinent: How many wills are there in the Godhead? One for the collectivity? One for each member of the Godhead (thus 3)? The additional will for the human nature of the Son brings this to a grand total of 5 wills. One begins to see how complicated Trinitarian thought can become when one attempts to press for logical and scriptural consistency. Unitarians have a simpler answer. The Holy Spirit, the Spirit of Truth, the Paraclete, the Advocate, the Comforter of John 14-17 is simply a personification of the Father and Son's abiding presence in the Christian community. Attributing independent will to the Spirit of Truth is an effective rhetorical feature within the overall personification of the spirit.

The God and Father of our Lord Jesus Christ

Three more illustrations of the NT's denial of the deity of Jesus should suffice. First, there is the repeated formula "God and Father of our Lord Jesus Christ" (Romans 15:6; 2 Corinthians 1:3; 11:31; Ephesians 1:3, 17; 1 Peter 1:3; and Revelation 1:6). The one God is "God" and "Father" and "Lord" of Jesus the "Lord." And this extends even to Jesus in his exalted state as risen, ascended, and returning Lord, as the above texts just referred to and as many of the previous texts we have discussed indicate. Second, Colossians 1:15 presents Jesus as both the "image of God" and the "firstborn of all creation." In context, the exalted Jesus is identified with wisdom, the power through which God created all things. Any pre-existence attributed to Jesus in Colossians is ideal or figurative based on the identification of the historic Jesus with previous personifications of wisdom.[17] The distinction between God and Jesus, however, is quite literal. Jesus' status is derived, dependent, and subsequent to the priority of God. There was a time when he was not. Third, echoing the Colossian passage is a statement attributed to Jesus in Revelation 3:14: "These things saith the Amen, the faithful and true witness, the beginning of the creation of God" (*KJV*). Here the exalted Jesus is identified with pre-existent wisdom, spoken of as the first created being in Proverbs 8:22, a passage that seems likely to be the source of the thought here expressed.[18] Jesus as "firstborn" and as "beginning of the creation of God" is no more eternal than he is omniscient. Hence, Jesus does not qualify as God, from a Unitarian perspective.

The title "God"

What, then, about the several NT passages (John 1:1,18; 20:28; Romans 9:5; Titus 2:13; 2 Peter 1:1; Hebrews 1:8; and possibly 1 John 5:20) that attribute the title "God" to Jesus? Unitarians have quick, plausible, and scriptural responses. The title "God" (Greek, theos) is often attributed to others in scripture. These are clearly not to be confused with the One God (e.g.: Moses in Exodus 4:16; the judges in John 10:34-35 and Psalm 82:6; David in Psalm 45:7; Satan in 2 Corinthians 4:4; idols in 1 Corinthians 8:4-6). The title is obviously not always meant in its full ontological sense. Calling someone "god" at minimum indicates that they are functioning in some representative sense as an authority to others. For example, in Psalm 45:7, when David is addressed as "god," it clearly is the language of the royal court conveying the idea that David as king represents God to the people. This, then, explains its association with Jesus in Hebrews 1:8. All other passages where Jesus receives the title "God" can be understood in a functional sense. There is no need to go beyond this, as some Trinitarians do, and suggest that the NT affirms the ontological equality of the Father and the Son.[19]

The absence of prayer and/or worship directed to the Holy Spirit.

A critical weakness in the Trinitarian position is the complete absence of prayer or worship directed to the Spirit. Granted, the NT often endorses prayer to God the Father in the name of Jesus by the power of the spirit (Romans 8:11-16, 26; 1 Corinthians 2:12; 6:11; 12:3; Galatians 3:3; 4:6; Ephesians 2:18; Philippians 3:3; and 1 John 4:13-15), but this is an entirely different function for the spirit than being an object of worship. Rather, the spirit is properly understood as the medium or power by which the believer approaches God in worship. The NT is completely silent regarding any worship of this power, except, perhaps, Simon the magician's disparaged attempt to purchase this power.

Acts 8:9-25

The account of Simon in Acts 8:9-25 provides an opportunity to digress once again and reflect upon the various translations and usages of S/spirit (pneuma). This we will do, but it should be of interest to note two more relevant facts concerning the S/spirit.

First, the earliest occurrence of any explicit worship of the Spirit is found in a late second century text, *The Martyrdom and Ascension of Isaiah*. It reads: "And he said to me, 'Worship him, for this is the angel of the Holy Spirit who has spoken in you and also in the other righteous.'"[20]

28   Chapter Two

Second, just prior to the formal and ecclesial induction of the Holy Spirit into the Godhead at the Council of Constantinople in 381 CE (where the Holy Spirit was explicitly acknowledged as worthy of worship alongside the Father and the Son) Gregory of Nazianzus made this illuminating remark:

> Of the wise men among ourselves, some have conceived of him [the Holy Spirit] as an activity, some as a creature, some as God; and some have been uncertain which to call him—and therefore neither worship him nor treat him with dishonor, but take up a neutral position.[21]

This citation demonstrates clearly the confusion many had concerning the H/holy S/spirit, a confusion that still persists today, as is evident from the inconsistencies among modern translators (as made evident in my Introduction), and warrants my four-fold approach of Unitarianism, Binitarianism, Trinitarianism, and Non-Sectarianism. This whole book aims to demonstrate that as in the year 380 (the year Gregory made this comment) thus in the year 2006. Confusion about translating the H/holy S/spirit remains!

Confusion regarding the S/spirit is certainly evident in the classic episode of Acts 8:9-25. This confusion, in my judgment, is not only apparent in the mind of one of the characters in the story (Simon) but also in various English translations and commentaries. Acts 8:18-20 reads: "When Simon saw that the Holy Spirit was conferred by the laying on of the apostles' hands, he offered them money and said, 'Give me this power too, so that anyone upon whom I lay my hands may receive the holy Spirit. But Peter said to him, 'May your money perish with you, because you thought that you could buy the gift of God with money" (*NAB*). In context, the "holy Spirit" (pneuma hagion) refers more to the effects that the S/spirit produces, than to the S/spirit itself. In my judgment, Usage 2 (as defined in the Introduction) is most appropriate here. The "spirit" is not a Person (i.e., God the Father or God the Holy Spirit) but a gift of spiritual presence and enablement. This seems clear from the plain meaning of verse 20 where Peter accuses Simon of attempting to purchase the "gift" of God with money. It seems ludicrous both for Simon and Peter to be contemplating that anyone is attempting to purchase "God."[22] Rather, it is the reception of the gift of God's presence and enablement that is in view here with an emphasis upon the enablement that the spirit provides. In order to make my point I need to articulate two things.

First, it seems appropriate to suggest that the "spirit" here is put for "the thing or manifestation" that the spirit makes possible. This may be understood as the figure of speech synecdoche or transfer, in this case where the whole is put for an associated part.[23] Second, and as contextual support for the alleged synecdoche, is the question of what was it that Simon "saw"? Certainly, Simon did not see "spirit" as by definition spirit is not visible. But it is clear that Simon saw some manifestation of the spirit and it seems likely that it was a specific manifestation. Acts 8:13 makes it clear that Simon was "beholding the miracles and signs which were done" (*KJV*) by Philip. So it makes sense to assume that when Simon "saw that through the laying on of the apostles' hands the Holy

Ghost was given" (KJV) that Simon "saw" something similar in kind to what had just been previously described. It seems to me, that if one were to speculate, the manifestation of speaking in tongues commends itself. Throughout the *Acts of the Apostles* the author has made the manifestation of speaking in tongues the defining initial manifestation and verification of the reception of the holy spirit whenever the preaching of the gospel broke into new ground (the Jews first in Acts 2:4; the Samaritans in Acts 8; the Gentiles in Acts 10 and 19).[24]

How have translators treated Acts 8:9-25, the account of Simon Magus? Interestingly, all 25 versions made a decision to uppercase Holy and Spirit (or Ghost) in each of its several occurrences, with the exception of the *NAB* making the choice to lower case holy. Going outside the 25 versions that I have been consulting, I found only the *New World Translation* (1961; Brooklyn: Watchtower Bible and Tract Society of Pennsylvania) lower casing both holy and spirit in these instances.

Absence of any polemic regarding the deity of the Spirit

One searches the NT in vain for any polemic regarding the deity of the Spirit. It simply does not appear as a matter of debate in the pages of the NT or among the writings of the earliest Church Fathers. The citation (above) by Gregory of Nazianzus in 380 CE regarding confusion about the holy spirit is evidence that the deity of the Spirit was a matter only called into focus after debates regarding the relation of the Father to the Son were "settled" at Nicea in 325 CE. It almost seems as if the "Holy Spirit" snuck into the Godhead when no one was looking or while the door of admission to the Godhead was still slightly ajar just shortly after Jesus was inducted. To Trinitarians this last remark might sound facetious, but it calls into question, from a Unitarian perspective, notions, advanced by Trinitarian theologians about the Holy Spirit being the "shy member" of the Trinity, the "faceless," "nameless," or "most invisibly effacing" member, and thus, perhaps, the only one capable of pulling off such a caper without detection (again, I admit that I am being facetious).[25] Nonetheless, Unitarians seem to be on sound ground on this point, even admitting that it is an argument from silence.

Passages which appear to present the Spirit as a separate person and/or equal in deity to the Father and/or Son

There are many passages in the NT where the Spirit may be viewed as a person separate from the Father and the Son and functioning in the capacity of deity. Unitarians argue that these passages are easily viewed this way only when one reads into the passages the very presupposition that the passages allegedly support. Unitarian interpreters recognize the overwhelming tendency of translators to most often capitalize both Holy (hagion) and Spirit (pneuma) thus lending their support to this bias. An exposition of a few representative texts should suffice to demonstrate how Unitarians harmonize apparent difficult passages with the clear teaching of scripture regarding the singular deity of God the Father.

Ephesians 4:30

Ephesians 4:30 is often cited as presenting the Spirit as a separate person and as deity. It reads: "And grieve not the holy Spirit of God, whereby ye are sealed unto the day of redemption" (*KJV*). Following the *KJV* in lower casing holy (hagion) are the *DR, KJ21, NAB, and, WB*. All other versions capitalized both Holy and Spirit. Paul's choice of the word "grieve" (Greek: lupeo) is best understood as a personification of God's gift of spiritual life and its attending empowerments. This seems clear from the context of 4:1-30. Unitarians are quick to admit that only a person is "grieved," but nowhere (else?) in Paul's writings is it clear that the "Spirit" is presented as a person distinct from the one God and Father of all. By "grieving" the holy spirit, God's impersonal gift of relationship and empowerment, one grieves the God (and Father) who gave this gift of spirit. Personification, or the figure of speech metonymy (where one thing, here holy spirit the gift, is put for another, here God the Father, the Giver) present themselves as the only viable interpretations.[26]

Matthew 28:19

One of the most frequently and popularly cited proof texts for the Trinity is Matthew 28:19.[27] It reads: "Go ye therefore, and teach all nations, baptizing them in the name of the Father, and of the Son, and of the Holy Ghost"(*KJV*). Clearly, there is one name mentioned and what might appear as three divine Persons (Father-Son-Holy Ghost/Spirit). On the surface, this text seems suggestive of Trinitarian doctrine, one name (essence) shared by Father-Son-Spirit (three persons). But upon closer scrutiny the Trinitarian interpretation fades.

Matthew's gospel is traditionally considered the most Jewish of the four canonical gospels.[28] Matthew shows respect for Jewish traditions (5:17-20; 10:5-6; and 15:1-10), an acceptance of the authority of the scribes and Pharisees (23:1-3), and adherence to Jewish notions of the holy spirit (1:19, 20; 3:11; 7:11; and 12:31-32). The burden of proof and argumentation rests upon those making the claim for a Trinitarian understanding of Matthew 28:19. Matthew has neither prepared his readers for any switch from a Jewish notion of holy spirit to a novel Christian Trinitarian revision nor indicated any hint of controversy or polemic concerning the matter. To read later Trinitarian developments into this passage is unwarranted.

The triadic formula in Matthew 28:19 (Father-Son-Spirit) is simply that, a triadic formula. The listing of 3 references, two of them clearly persons (Father and Son), does not necessitate that the 3rd reference is also to a person. Matthew's formula is liturgical and baptismal. Matthew simply adds the baptismal gift of spirit to the invocation of the name of Father and Son. This view is in harmony with Matthew's prior teaching on the spirit (1:19-20; 3:11; 7:11; and 12:31-32). Further support for this view is provided when one reflects upon many other triads in the NT that mention the Father and the Son but then add an additional element that clearly is not in the category of deity (Mark 8:38; Matthew 24:36; 2 Thessalonians 1:7-8; 1 Timothy 5:21; Revelation 1:1-2; 3:5; and 14:10). Schaberg (1982) provides evidence and plausible argumentation for the development of monadic confessional formulas (focusing upon just Jesus) developing into binitarian confessional formulas (focusing upon the Father and Jesus, most often in the context of pagan disputes) developing into triadic confessional formulas.[29] By the time of Matthew's gospel (approx. 80-90 CE) the baptismal formula which earlier had been "in the name of Jesus" (Acts 2:38; 8:16; 10:48; 19:5; and 22:16) had developed into a triadic confessional formula. Although the *Didache* provides evidence that the Father-Son-Spirit baptismal formula was in use in the late first century, it is interesting to note that no Church Father cites Matthew 28:19 with the triadic formula, rather they appear to amend it to "in the name of Jesus."[30]

Further support for Matthew 28:19 being viewed as a development beyond the time of Jesus and his earliest followers is the evidence provided from Matthew 7:11. "If ye then, being evil, know how to give good gifts unto your children, how much more shall our Father which is in heaven give **good things** to them that ask him?" (*KJV*). I have put **good things** in bold in order to call your attention to the likely possibility that this represents the original thought as found in the hypothetical Q document. Luke 11:13 renders the "good things" (Greek, agatha) of Matthew 7:11 as "holy Spirit" (Greek, pneuma hagion; *NAB*), thus suggesting that the concept of "holy spirit" began to displace or be used as a cipher for God's blessings with Luke's redaction of this Q passage.

How have our versions translated Matthew 28:19? Interestingly, all the versions that I consulted translated hagion pneuma (H/holy S/spirit) as Holy Spirit or as Holy Ghost all upper case, with the exception of the *NAB* which lower cased holy. Of further interest is the decision on the part of the *CEV, GNT, NASB, NLT,* and *WEB* to omit the "of" preceding "the Son" and "the Spirit," apparently to strengthen the notion of the unity of the three, Father, Son, and Spirit. The other versions, rightfully in my judgment, included the "of," an inclusion mandated by the presence of the definite article preceding both Son and Spirit in the Greek text. The *MSG* also deviated from the above patterns rendering the critical phrase, "baptism in the threefold name: Father, Son, and Holy Spirit." Going outside my list of English versions, I discovered that the *New World Translation* and the *Scholars Version* (1993: *The Five Gospels*, edited by Funk and Hoover) both lower cased holy and spirit.

Matthew 3:11 & Luke 3:15

Another "Q" passage, revealing signs of development similar to the previous discussion concerning Matthew 7:11 and Luke 11: 13, is found in Matthew 3:11 and/or Luke 3:15 and concerns John the Baptist's prediction of the one coming after him who would "baptize in holy Spirit and fire" (NAB). Some interpreters suggest that "holy Spirit" here is "referring to God's apocalyptic action" and "could have meant 'in holy wind and fire,' i.e. with devastating hurricanes and bolts of lightning, as acts of God in judgment."[31] These interpreters suggest that this apocalyptic concept of "holy spirit" developed into the concept of the 'Spirit' associated with the early Jesus movement but was "not yet as advanced as the Trinitarian associations suggested by 'the Holy Spirit.'"[32]

2 Corinthians 13:14

One final reference should suffice for this brief but focused tour through typical Unitarian apologetics. Often Trinitarian interpreters cite Paul's lovely benediction in 2 Corinthians 13:14 "the grace of the Lord Jesus Christ, and the love of God, and the communion of the Holy Ghost, be with you all. Amen" (*KJV*). It sounds Trinitarian and could be argued for as a Trinitarian proof text in a manner similar to Matthew 28:19. There are three references, one to Jesus the Son, one to God (the Father), and one to the Holy Ghost (or Spirit). It is a liturgical blessing and thus gives one a sense of the presence of these three (divine?) realities. But are there really three divine persons here?

Certainly, Jesus is a person and divine grace is said to proceed from him. But it seems a stretch to deify Jesus on the basis of this verse. Couldn't Jesus simply function as the "mediator" of God's grace? One need not look too far into the NT for such evidence (consider 1 Timothy 2:5). And, Why is Jesus mentioned here before God the Father? Is this evidence of the monadic, bipartite, and tripartite developments mentioned earlier.

Now, concerning the phrase, "the love of God." Is this God's (the Father's?) love for us, or is it our love for him? The grammar here is ambiguous and could be read either way. If it is a reference to our love for God, then the triadic symmetry of grace, love, and communion coming from three divine persons appears broken. Certainly no major Christian dogma should be built upon an ambiguous text. Furthermore, the "communion of the Holy Ghost" also is susceptible to more than one interpretation. Is this the communion (Greek, koinonia) that **comes** from the Holy Spirit (God the Third Person)? Or, is this the communion that **results** from holy spirit, the common spiritual enablement that all believers possess? Trinitarians opt for the former and Unitarians opt for the latter. It seems that this verse must be left out of the discussion, at least in terms of use as a proof text. This, of course, is the Unitarian position on all the texts previously discussed and would be the approach taken with regard to the many verses that time and space have not allowed for here.

Your patience and consideration during this presentation on Unitarian perspectives has been appreciated. As we now turn to the Binitarian, Trinitarian, and Non-Sectarian perspectives your continued patience and consideration is solicited as I intend to argue these perspectives as persuasively and as positively as my abilities permit.

Notes

1. According to Geoffry Wigoner, "Holy Spirit," in *The Encyclopedia of the Jewish Religion*, RJ Zwi Werblowsky, editor, (New York: Aduma Books, 1986), Jews understand that the holy spirit is "more or less synonymous with God (Is. 63:10) or else signifies His sustaining and inspiring presence (Is. 63:11; Ps. 51:13)," 190.
2. This point is persuasively argued by J. B. Henderson, *The Construction of Orthodoxy and Heresy: Neo-Confucianism, Islamic, Jewish, and Early Christian Patterns*. (Albany: State University of NewYork, 1988), 103-05. R. P. C. Hanson, *The Search for the Christian Doctrine of God* (Edinburgh. T & T Clark, 1988), 181-202, provides a lengthy discussion of the semantic confusion regarding the following key Greek and Latin terms of Trinitarian discussion: ousia; hypostasis; prosopon; persona; substantia; homousia; and homoiousia.
3. The Gospel of John is more suggestive of this than any other NT document. Consider the following passages: 1:1, 14, 18, 30; 3:13, 16-18, 31; 6:41, 48, 51; 7:28; 8:23-24, 36, 42, 58; 10:38; 14:6; 16:28; 17:1-5. Illustrations of the various ways in which God is presented as Father are found on pages 67-68.
4. This is explicit in Luke 1:35: "And the angel said to her in reply, 'the holy Spirit will come upon you, and the power of the Most High will overshadow you. Therefore the child to be born will be called holy, the Son of God" (*NAB*). According to this verse, Jesus is "Son of God" as to his human nature. Note also that "holy Spirit" is in parallel to "the power of the Most High." This is clearly Usage 2. Concurring is R. E. Brown, *The Birth of the Messiah* (Garden City: Doubleday, 1977), 289-91 and 311-16.
5. 4:3; my paraphrase. Here and elsewhere when I indicate that I am attempting my own paraphrase or translation, the Greek text is based on John Kohlenberger III, *The Precise Parallel New Testament* (New York: Oxford University, 1995).
6. Isaiah 42:8 declares: "I am the Lord; this is my name; my glory I give to no other" (*NAB*).
7. Often, Trinitarian interpreters concede: "The NT does not contain the developed doctrine of the Trinity." See Stafford J. Wright, "God." in *The New International Dictionary of New Testament Theology, Vol. 2*, editor: Colin Brown (Grand Rapids: Zondervan, 1976), 84.
8. The point is argued on the side of Unitarianism by Greg Stafford, *JW's Defended: An Answer to Scholars and Critics*. Second Edition, (Huntington Beach: Elihu Books, 2000). Larry Hurtado, *One God, One Lord: Early Christian Devotion and Ancient Monotheism* (Minneapolis: Fortress, 2003), argues for an initial or minimum binitarianism that eventually becomes Trinitarian.
9. These distinctions find support in the following: Hans Bietenhard, "Lord." Pp.510-19 in *New International Dictionary of the New Testament, Volume 2*, Colin Brown, editor,

(Grand Rapids: Eerdmans, 1976-78), 508-519, esp. 511; Robert Grant, *Gods and the One God* (Philadelphia: Westminster, 1986), 48-49; A. S. Aglen, "Lord," in *Hastings Dictionary of the Bible,* Vol. 3, James Hastings, editor, (New York: Charles Scribner's Sons, 1963), 137; and, K. Spronk, "Lord," in *Dictionary of Deities and Demons in the Bible* , Karel van der Toorn, Bob Becking & Peter W. vanderHorst. Editors, (Grand Rapids:Eerdmans, 1999), 531.

10. See Exodus 4:16; Psalm 82:6; and John 10:34. This oft made distinction between the ontological and the functional sense of God seems appropriate here and would be stressed in Unitarian interpretation.

11. The Greek word for "head" is "kephale." Kephale appears interchangeable with the Greek kurios, the word normally translated "lord." God, then, is the "Lord" of Jesus. See W. F. Arndt & F. W. Gingrich, *A Greek-English Lexicon of the New Testament*, 2nd ed., rev. Frederick W. Danker (Chicago: Univ. of Chicago Press, 1979), 431. Jesus may be "lord of lords" (Revelation 17:14) with regard to all other lords, the Father excepted. But, from a Unitarian perspective, only the Father is "God of gods and Lord of lords" (Deuteronomy 10:17) in an absolute sense.

12. Cf. J. D. G. Dunn, *Christology in the Making* (Philadelphia: Westminster, 1980), 114-21. Dunn argues for an Adam-Christology here. He interprets the "in the form of God" (Philippians 2:6; KJV) as a reference, not to Jesus' pre-existence, but to Adam, the one originally made "in the form of God."

13. Here and elsewhere when I indicate that I am attempting my own paraphrase or translation, the Greek text is based on John Kohlenberger III, *The Precise Parallel New Testament* (New York: Oxford University, 1995).

14. Bietenhard, "Lord," 515. Admittedly, Bietenhard's comment can be interpreted either in a Unitarian or in a Trinitarian direction.

15. Bruce J. Malina and Richard L. Rohrbaugh, *A Social-Science Commentary on the Synoptic Gospels* (Minneapolis: Fortress, 1992), 244.

16. Rudolph Schnackenburg, *The Gospel of John, Volume 1*, (New York: Herder & Herder, 1968), 494-506, provides a detailed discussion of notions of pre-existence in ancient Jewish and early Christian thought. Among these notions is the concept of ideal pre-existence. One pertinent example he offers is from the *Community Rule Scroll* of the Dead Sea Community. It reads: "From the God of knowledge comes all that is and will be. Before they were, he established their whole design; and when they exist, according to their fixed laws, they fulfill their work according to his glorious design, unalterably" (496). Jesus' statement in John 6:38 is easily comprehended by this notion of pre-existence.

17. Cf. Dunn, *Christology in the Making*, 187-94.

18. So *ibid.*, 247.

19. A. E. Harvey, *Jesus and the Constraints of History* (Philadelphia: Westminster, 1982), provides the best argument I know of for this position. Harvey states: "The New Testament writers...are insistent about the absolute oneness of God, and show no tendency to describe Jesus in terms of divinity," 157. His book ends with this comment: "I would not wish to deny that the seeds of a later Christology are present in the New Testament, nor that the subsequent doctrine of the divinity of Christ may have been a proper or even inevitable development. I am concerned only to show that there is no unambiguous evidence that the constraint of monotheism was effectively broken by any New Testament writer" 178.

20. Cited in R. H. Charlesworth, *The Old Testament Pseudepigrapha,Volume 2*, (New York: Doubleday, 1985), 172. Millard J. Erickson, *God in Three Persons: A Contemporary Interpretation of the Trinity*, (Grand Rapids: Baker, 1995), 324-25, notes that invo-

cations to the Holy Spirit are found in the 3rd century *Acts of Thomas* but admits that explicit and mainstream worship of the Holy Spirit seems absent until after Constantinople in 381 CE. As an additional point of interest some early Christian leaders forbade the worship of the Spirit. See R. P. C. Hanson, *The Search for the Christian Doctrine of God* (Edinburgh: T & T Clark, 1988), 741.

21. Cited in Jarislov Pelikan, *A History of the Development of Doctrine, Volume 1*, (Chicago: Chicago University Press, 1971), 213. *The Catechism of the Catholic Church* (Ligouri"Ligouri Publications, 1994), 193, states: "On the day of Pentecost when the seven weeks of Easter had come to an end, Christ's Passover is fulfilled in the outpouring of the Holy Spirit, manifested, given, and communicated as a divine person: . . .On that day, the Holy Trinity is fully revealed." Although "fully" revealed, it took four centuries for the Church to formalize this doctrine. Revealed or not, ample confusion persisted.

22. Although purchasing "God" is absolutely ludicrous and seems inconceivable, purchasing something that is a gift from God within the realm of human activity is conceivable and appears to be what Simon is attempting to do. Even so, Peter's response in verse 20-23 is best understood as the figure of speech apodioxis or detestation, an expression of feeling by way of detestation. See E. W. Bullinger, *Figures of Speech Used in the Bible* (Grand Rapids: Baker, 1968, reprint of 1898 original), 935.

23. See Bullinger, *Figures of Speech Used in the Bible*, 612-656, esp. 635-640. This suggestion responds to F. Dale Bruner's complaint in *A Theology of the Holy Spirit: The Pentecostal Witness and the New Testament Witness* (Grand Rapids: Eerdmans, 1970), 175n[22], "I am unable to find convincing, though it is plausible, the argument which sees reference here only to charismatic gifts or manifestations of the Spirit and not to the Holy Spirit *simpliciter*" (italics original).

24. Bruner, *ibid*, 173-88, makes a good argument for understanding the initial sign as water baptism. At the initial reception of the gospel by each individual group the author makes it clear that water baptism is administered. This perspective is more thorough in its suggestion as it includes the Ethiopian Eunuch, a proselyte, in Acts 8:26-40, of whom we are told that he was baptized, but nothing is mentioned regarding speaking in tongues.

25. Representative of these approaches or emphases in understanding the Holy Spirit from a Trinitarian perspective are: F. Dale Bruner and William E. Hordern, *The Holy Spirit: The Shy Member of the Trinity*, (Minneapolis : Augsburg, 1984) and Killian McDonnell, *The Other Hand of God: The Holy Spirit as the Universal Touch and Goal* (Minnesota: Liturgical Press Collegeville, 2003), 1-10.

26. See Bullinger, *Figures of Speech Used in the Bible*, 538-608.

27. Craig Blomberg, *Matthew: The New American Commentary, Volume 22* (Nashville: Broadman, 1992) is representative. He states: "Here is the clearest Trinitarian 'formula' anywhere in the Gospels," 432.

28. Cf. R. E. Brown, *Introduction to the New Testament: Anchor Bible Reference Library* (New York: Doubleday, 1997), 211.

29. See Jane Schaberg, *The Father, The Son, and The Holy Spirit: SBL Dissertation Series 61* (Chico: Scholars Press, 1982), 45-50.

30. *Didache* 7:3, dated to about 100 CE, reads: "baptize in running water in the name of the Father and of the Son and of the holy Spirit" cited in Edgar J. Goodspeed, *The Apostolic Fathers* (New York: Harper & Brothers, 1950), 14. For evidence on the Church Fathers and their use of Matthew 28:19 see Victor Paul Wierwille, *Receiving the Holy Spirit Today* (New Knoxville: The Way), 246. Schaberg, *The Father, The Son, and The Holy Spirit*, suggests that the triad of Matthew 28:19 is best understood as a midrashic development of the triad of Ancient of days, son of man, and holy angels as found in Daniel 7:13-14 and parallels.

31. James M. Robinson, Paul Hoffman, and John S. Kloppenborg, editors, *The Sayings Gospel Q in Greek and English with Parallels form the Gospels of Mark and Thomas* (Minneapolis: Fortress, 2002). 70.
32. James M. Robinson, et. al, *ibid*, 71.

Chapter Three
The Binitarian Model

My presentation of the Binitarian model is in three parts. First, I set forth a brief summary of the position. Second, I expand upon several of the arguments supporting this model. And, third, I provide an exegesis of several relevant key texts.

Brief Summary of the Binitarian Position

The NT is much clearer about the deity of Jesus, the Son, than it is regarding the deity of the Spirit. Thus, for Binitarians, the Godhead is two in person, one in substance. Binitarians, like Unitarians, view the spirit as an impersonal force, power, or presence when the spirit is justifiably presented as "distinct" from God, the Father. Thus, much of what was argued regarding the spirit in the previous chapter on Unitarianism would be applicable here. Binitarians, however, differ from Unitarians (and Trinitarians) in that the spirit, in some passages, is best understood as a way of speaking about the union of the Father and the Son without necessitating the hypothesis of a separate hypostasis for the spirit (contra the Trinitarian position).

Although there are triadic formulas in the NT and early tradition which consist of Father, Son, and spirit, these do not constitute as compelling an argument for the Trinitarian position as the many Binitarian formulas do for the Binitarian position. Furthermore, both the NT and early traditional material bear witness to a polemic regarding two powers in heaven (rather than three) and thus make the Binitarian position more plausible as the representative position of the apostles and the early church.

Finally, the full deity of Jesus is often argued for even apart from any clear and explicit affirmation or propositional statement found in scripture and/or tradition. The reason for this is based on the theological implications of the clear and explicit teaching of the NT that Jesus died on the cross as a ransom (Mark 10:45; 1 Timothy 2:6) and/or as an expiation/propitiation for sin (Romans 3:25; 1 John 2:2; 4:10). If Jesus' death is understood as a ransom (payment) and an expiation/propitiation (cleansing/appeasement) for sin, then the status or value of his sacrifice must be equal to the juridical demand. Since it was God's infinite holiness that was injured by human sinfulness, a sufficient satisfaction of this injury could only be met by one whose status was equal to that infinite holiness. Thus, Jesus must, in addition to being fully human, be fully God as well. Only one who is truly human *should* pay for human sinfulness. Only one who is truly God *could*. This view is argued by St. Anselm of Canterbury, in his *Why the God-Man?* (Latin:*Cur Deus Homo?*), published in the 11th century. Furthermore, Binitarians argue, since the NT presents Jesus as the revelation of God (John 1:18 and Hebrews 1:1-2) he must therefore be God. The underlying theological principle here is that only God can fully reveal God. If Jesus is not the full, final, and definitive revelation of God, then humanity yet awaits this revelation and Christianity's claim to uniqueness dissipates.

An Expansion of the Above Arguments

Binitarian Formulas

Binitarian formulas abound in the NT and "trump" the so-called Trinitarian or triadic formulas.[1] If the NT authors conceived of the Spirit as a divine person, distinct from the Father and the Son and worthy of equal glory and honor, then why is the Spirit so often left out (there are over 40 some passages listed in footnote 1 below)? Many of the key triadic passages (see also footnote 1) were examined in the previous chapter on Unitarianism and found wanting in terms of clear support for the doctrine of the Trinity. The concern of this chapter is to provide a defense for Binitarianism. Hence, we begin with an examination of selected Binitarian texts.

Most (non-Unitarian) commentators agree that the clearest affirmations of the deity of Jesus are to be found in John's gospel. Jesus is presented in John's gospel as the incarnate Word of God (1:14). Therefore, the assumption is that Jesus is eternally pre-existent (1:1, 18; 3:13; 8:58; and 17:5). Unitarians argue (as developed in the previous chapter) that Jesus' pre-existence was either "ideal," or if "real," then Jesus was the first spirit being to have been created. Unitarians argue that the teaching regarding the creation of "wisdom" (the OT parallel concept to the NT "Word") in Proverbs 8:22-23, and the teaching regarding Jesus as "firstborn" and "the beginning of the creation of God" in Colossians 1:15 and Revelation 3:14, point to a non-eternal and thus non-divine Jesus. How do Binitarians respond?

Proverbs 8:22-23; Colossians 1:15; and Revelation 3:14

First off, all three passages (Proverbs 8, Colossians 1, and Revelation 3) are susceptible to alternative interpretations that mitigate Unitarian objections. For example, the critical Hebrew words (qanah and nasak) in Proverbs 8:22-23 that "seem" to state that wisdom was "created," are fluid enough in their range of meanings to allow for other possibilities.[2] One should also consider that the literary atmosphere is poetic and metaphorical. Even if the Hebrew of Proverbs 8 demands the sense of "created," one should not press it's meaning literally. Wisdom is simply a personification of God's immanent presence and creative activity. Not so with John's gospel. The atmosphere of John is realistic and historical/literal. The Word became flesh as a real person, Jesus of Nazareth. This person is presented as one who was distinct from the Father yet existed alongside the Father throughout all eternity (John 1:1 and 17:5). But was he God in the full sense that his Father is God? I will return to this critical question after responding to the previous questions concerning Colossians 1 and Revelation 3.

The key terms/phrases in Colossians and Revelation are "firstborn" (Greek, prototokos) and "beginning of the creation of God" (Greek, he arche tes ktiseos tou theou). Both passages appear to be attributing to Jesus categories of thought or existence attributed to wisdom in the OT. Hence, what was just mentioned regarding the distinction between the literary personification of wisdom, and the literal person of Jesus in the previous paragraph, is applicable here. Furthermore, neither "firstborn" (prototokos), nor "the beginning" (he arche), mandate that Jesus is a creature. Both terms may be understood in terms of priority in rank rather than priority in time and both terms are also used of God in Hebrew tradition.[3]

I now return to the underlying principle supporting Binitarianism (and Trinitarianism), namely, that only God can fully reveal God. This seems to be the heart and soul of the Christian religion and without it Christianity presents itself as merely a variant form of Judaism. Two texts, John 1:18 and Hebrews 1:1-2, are supportive of this underlying principle. Hence, we take a quick look at these passages.

John 1:18

John 1:18 reads: "No one has ever seen God. The only Son, God, who is at the Father's side, has revealed him" (*NAB*). In this verse Jesus is called "God." By itself, as we have already argued, this doesn't make Jesus "ontologically" God. One might take the assertion of John 1:18 in a functional sense, that is to say that Jesus functions as the one who represents God to us and/or, as the verse goes on to say, reveals God. But this is precisely the point in Binitarian and/or Trinitarian understanding. If the theological principle, "only God can (fully) reveal God," has any validity, then Jesus "must" be fully and ontologically God in order to fully reveal God. Otherwise, as previously noted, we are yet awaiting some full disclosure of God. Christianity, then, takes its place alongside so many other religions offering simply a limited but (hopefully) an appreciated and unique glimpse into the divine reality.

Thus, it seems, that one's interpretation of John 1:18 rests upon one's acceptance and/or rejection of the underlying theological principle in question.

But what does this principle rest upon? Initially, there is an intuitive appeal in the notion that "only God can reveal God" and that "if Jesus is not fully God, then we yet await a full disclosure of God." Yet, it seems that, in the final analysis, the entire principle rests upon the faith and conviction of those who endorse it. This does not provide much help to those looking for explicit biblical support for their beliefs, but at least it provides clarity for respectful communications among and between Unitarians, Binitarians, Trinitarians, and Non-Sectarians. At minimum, the Unitarian can inform the Binitarian and/or Trinitarian that they believe what John 1:18 states apart from the underlying principle that Binitarians and Trinitarians utilize to "make" it say what they want it to, or better put, what their tradition has come to understand it to mean.

Before leaving John 1:18, it is important to note that one of its key phrases, "the only Son, God," represents a translation of one of four textual variants competing for the original of this verse.[4] Although it does seem to be the preferred variant, even without the explicit labeling of Jesus as "God," John 1:18 upholds this notion in that Jesus "revealed" God (the other key phrase). The Greek word translated "revealed" is exegeso. This verb is based on two roots, ex or ek, meaning "out of," and ago, meaning "to lead." The idea here is that Jesus leads one out of ignorance or darkness concerning God into a true understanding. In context, Jesus is said to be "at the Father's side." The Greek word for "side" here is kolpon, literally, "bosom." Hence, intimacy and relationship are in view in this verse. Jesus, then, leads one out of alienation from God into intimacy with God. He does so based on his own intimacy. One's evaluation of Jesus' intimacy certainly will effect one's evaluation of how well Jesus can deliver. As a mere creature, or human, Jesus' capacity to provide is limited. As "true God of true God" his capacity to provide reconciliation between humans and God is unlimited. This is the appeal of the Binitarian (and Trinitarian) interpretive perspective.

Hebrews 1:1-2

Another significant passage, containing theological implications similar to John 1:18, is Hebrews 1:1-2. It reads: "In time past, God spoke in partial and various ways to our ancestors through the prophets; in these last days he spoke to us through a son. . ." (*NAB*). A comparative contrast is being made in this verse between God's prior and progressive revelation through the prophets with his final and full disclosure in one characterized as a son. Supportive of this suggested comparison are the following observations: (1) the first of the two occurrences of "spoke" represents the Greek lalesas, a present participle connoting progressive, ongoing, and incomplete communication; (2) the force of this present participle fits well with the phrase "partial and various ways." In Greek, the phrase is "*p*olymeros kai *p*olytropos." (3) this phrase is an attention-getter for a couple of reasons: (a) both adverbs begin with the letter "*p*" (pi in Greek), setting up an elaborate two-verse alliteration ("time past"=Greek *p*alai; "ancestors"=Greek *p*atrisin; "prophets"=Greek *p*rophetes; and "in"=Greek e*p*); (b) the poly(u) in both words connotes the idea of "many" or "various"; and, (c) Menos=parts or portions, whereas tropos=method or means. Hence, the idea is that God, in times past, had been utilizing many and various means or methods to say this, that, or the other, consisting of bits of information of varying importance, in a progressive, ongoing, and incomplete fashion. For example, God made promises of land and posterity to Abraham, and kingdom and dynasty to David. He revealed law and liturgy to Moses. He instructed his people concerning social justice through the prophets and provided wisdom for daily living through the sages. But, in the sense of the meaning I am developing here for Hebrews 1:1-2, God, even in and through all these wonderful revelations, had not *really* or *fully* communicated all that was on his heart or his mind. He saved that communication for the coming of his son, Jesus Christ; and, (4) in the second occurrence of "spoke" (Hebrews 1:2), one finds the Greek verb elalasen. This is the aorist form of the verb. The aorist refers to action without reference to its duration.[5] Hence, in contrast with the previous "spoke" (the present participle), this "spoke" speaks of completion, fullness, or finality. If Jesus Christ is God's last word (recall "in these last days" from verse 2) then whatever it is that God wants us to know of himself has been revealed. But, if Jesus Christ is not God, then God remains only partially revealed, and no further or definitive revelation yet awaits us. Binitarians (and Trinitarians) argue that in Jesus Christ God is revealed fully, finally, and definitively. Unitarians would argue that in Jesus Christ God is revealed in so far as God can be revealed, given God's chosen but created, limited, and finite instruments of revelation. Herein lies a significant difference between the two views.

A further reflection may add force to the above exegeses of John 1:18 and Hebrews 1:1-2. It is not just "information" about God that Jesus brings. No. It is "performation." Jesus, as God's agent, performs the definitive act whereby God communicates his love for us. Dozens of scriptural illustrations come to mind. Here are three, carefully chosen to illustrate the point: (1) "For God so loved the world that he gave his only Son" (John 3:16; *NAB*); (2) "But God proves his love for us in that while we were still sinners Christ died for us" (Romans 5:8; *NAB*); and, (3) "In this is love: not that we loved God, but that he loved us and sent his Son as expiation for our sins" (1 John 4:10; *NAB*). If God's love is expressed *through* Christ, then to the extent that Christ is also God to that extent we have a revelation of His love. Do we have a full or a partial revelation of God's love? If any self-sacrifice was involved, and truly the crucifixion of Christ seems to be the epitome of vicarious self-sacrifice, then it is to Christ, the one performing the deed of love, that the believer feels indebted. How can one not put Christ on a par with God, in terms of gratitude and in terms of reciprocal love? Is one to set Jesus aside, once reconciled to God the Father? Doesn't it seem that Christ has truly done more for the Christian than the Father? The Father stayed in comfort, in heaven. The Son was sent as God's agent of revelation and salvation. Binitarians (and Trinitarians) base their interpretive conclusions not so much on the explicit words of scripture, as do Unitarians, but on the implicit meanings that the words of scripture compel them to consider. Scripture may not "say" clearly and explicitly that Jesus is God in the full ontological sense that the Father is God, but this seems to be what Binitarians (and Trinitarians) have heard when they reflect on what God has "spoken" (Hebrews 1:1-2). Although God (the Father) is the *object* of Christian faith, Christ, as the revelation of the Father, is the *content*.

This brings me to another plank of the Binitarian argument. As just argued, it is not so much that the words of scripture teach that Jesus is unequivocally God, it is that the teaching of scripture, taken as a whole, in the full context and consideration of the nature of the events (the cross-resurrection-gift of spirit) that mediate God's revelation and become the conceptual field for religious experience, leads one to conclude that Jesus is God. This brings us to an area of investigation that has recently been under scrutiny, namely, worship. How did early Christian worship negotiate the relationship between the Son and the Father?

Early Christian Worship

Several practices of the early Christian church, as discerned through the pages of scripture, when understood collectively, mount a formidable argument supporting the later church's decision to declare that Jesus is "true God of true God." Among these practices are: prayer; invocation; confession; baptism; the Lord's Supper; and, hymns of praise to God and/or Christ.[6]

Although the NT, for the most part, instructs that prayer is to be made to God through Christ, there are, nonetheless, instances when prayer is actually addressed to Jesus. An instance when prayer seems addressed to both the Father and the Son is found in 1 Thessalonians 3:11: "Now God himself and our Father, and our Lord Jesus Christ, direct our way unto you" (*KJV*). Similarly, but in reverse order, 2 Thessalonians 2:16-17 states: "Now our Lord Jesus Christ himself, and God, even our Father, which hath loved us, and hath given us everlasting consolation and good hope through grace, comfort your hearts, and stablish you in every good word and work" (KJV). 2 Corinthians 12:8-9 seems to portray Paul as directing his prayer to Jesus ("the Lord"?) three times to have his "thorn in the flesh" removed. Stephen, the first Christian martyr, calls upon Jesus in prayer just prior to succumbing to death (Acts 7:59-60). 1 Corinthians 16:22 contains what appears to be an early "two word" prayer of the church. In most versions, these two words are preserved in the language of the first Christians, namely, Aramaic. The words are "marana tha," translated as "Come O Lord" (*NIV*).

The confession of Romans 10:9-10 is basic to Christian self-understanding. One is to confess Jesus as Lord and believe that God raised him from the dead. Paul interprets this confession against the background of Joel 3:5 (compare Joel 3:5 with Romans 10:13) where one is to "call upon the name of the Lord" for salvation. It seems that early Christian devotion to Jesus had no problem adapting or adopting the language of Jewish devotion to Yahweh and applying it in their reverence, veneration, or worship of Jesus.

The two central rituals of early Christian worship further contribute to the Binitarian argument. Baptism was most often "in the name of Jesus" (cf. Acts 2:38; 8:16; 10:48; 19:5; and especially Romans 6:3). Again, this seems to apply to Jesus categories of worship and commitment that previously had been reserved for Yahweh. The celebration of the cultic meal (the Lord's Supper) also is suggestive of Jesus' exalted status in a manner that is comparable with that of Yahweh in the OT. In 1 Corinthians 10:18 and 22, Paul mentions OT sacrificial worship, abuse, and judgment in a manner that sets up a comparison with the NT sacrificial worship, abuse, and judgment. The two "Lords" (Yahweh and Jesus) appear presented in parallel fashion.

Finally, there is the practice of singing praises or hymns to God and to Christ. Several NT passages reflect the early Christian practice of singing hymns either to God or to Christ or to both.[7] But even if one decides that the early Christian hymns of praise are not directly *to* Jesus, they are at least to God *through* him. As argued above, with the understanding that even though God (the Father) is the object of worship and praise, Christ is certainly the content. Hence, hymnic praise offered to God *through* Jesus just might as well be *to* Jesus as Jesus' act of redemption is at the heart of Christian celebration. Theological hairsplitting, attempts to "separate" the Father and the Son in Christian devotion, seems insulting to Binitarian reflection on the cross. On the one hand, Binitarians are eager to uphold the clear biblical teaching of monotheism. On the other hand, they are just as eager to avoid the charge of polytheism. The worship of both Father and Son, which here is argued as a part of early Christian practice, would be polytheistic, unless one resolves the dilemma by means of the binitarian formula. Christians are eternally indebted to Jesus and love him with all their heart. Why make them choose between Father and Son, in terms of the one to whom they are utmost devoted? Binitarians avoid this problem with their doctrine of one God, two persons.

The Spirit in Binitarianism

But what about the Spirit? In the next chapter, I will develop the Trinitarian argument for the inclusion of the Spirit in the Godhead. Here, it may suffice to develop further the Binitarian's reasons for rejecting the notion of a third person. Most of these reasons are shared with the Unitarian position.

Clearly, as mentioned in the previous chapter, the NT contains neither polemic regarding the doctrine of the deity of the spirit nor any hint of the practice of the worship of the spirit. Although an argument from silence, it seems that the "burden of proof" would be upon those making the claim that early Christians had such a doctrine or engaged in such a practice. Furthermore, there is extra-biblical evidence that by the late first or early second century there was debate concerning "two powers in heaven."[8] The fact that there is no mention concerning "three powers" until the late fourth century should give Trinitarians pause. Finally, passages "seeming" to portray the Spirit as a person are easily managed or reduced to notions of literary personification. Perhaps the most telling example is that of the "Paraclete" of John's gospel often thought to be the summit of NT pneumatology.[9] If the "person" of the spirit as "Paraclete" weakens upon closer scrutiny, then, assuming that the Paraclete concept is the summit of NT pneumatology, so would any other NT instance of the personification or hypostatization of the spirit (e.g.: Matthew 28:18-20; Acts 5:3-4; 13:2; 15:28; Romans 8:26-27; 2 Corinthians 13:14; and Ephesians 4:30). Hence, I conclude this chapter with a few comments about the background and context of the Paraclete.

The Paraclete of John's Gospel

The Paraclete passages in John's gospel are: 14:16, 26; 15:26; and 16:7. These are all found in the larger context of Jesus' Farewell Discourse.[10] The term "Paraclete" is a transliteration of the Greek word paracletos. This word is variously translated in our English versions. For example: Comforter in the *ASV, KJV, WBS* and *YLT*; Advocate in the *WNT* and *NAB*; Helper in the *BBE, NASB,* and *GNT*; Intercessor in the *AMP*; Counselor in the *WEB, NLV, NLT,* and *RSV*; and Friend in the *MSG*. The etymology of the term and its precise meaning are matters of some debate but it is generally agreed that the term is used for one who "assists" another in some way.[11] The social-scientific model of the patron-client relationship seems helpful as a way to understand how the Paraclete functions in John's gospel.[12] Hence, I digress to explain this model.

In the ancient world, patrons were those who owned or controlled the goods and services needed by clients. Critical in gaining access to needed goods, and to insuring that those goods were "needed," were the brokers. Essentially, brokers were the go-betweens, having some "in" with both patrons and clients. Religiously, God was the ultimate patron, providing covenant, law, blessing, wisdom and so on. Israel was God's chief client. Several individuals throughout Jewish history could be viewed at times as brokers (Abraham; Moses; David). Jesus presents himself, particularly in John's gospel, as God's "broker." We will return to the presentation of Jesus as God's broker in John's gospel following this brief but supplementary illustration of brokerage from Luke's gospel.

Luke 7:1-10 is the familiar episode of a Roman centurion who, having heard of Jesus' healing powers, sought to have Jesus effect a cure for one of his slaves. Yet, he did not deem it necessary for Jesus to come to his home in order to perform the cure. Rather, he sent word to Jesus to simply give the word, as he was "not worthy to have Jesus come under his roof" (verse 6). He reasoned that Jesus could simply give the word and his slave would be healed. He reasoned that Jesus, like himself, was one who exercised or brokered the authority of a patron (in the centurion's case, the emperor; in Jesus' case, God) and could accomplish this with a simple command. The centurion appears to have brokered the building of a synagogue for Capernaum Jews (verse 5). Jesus was impressed with the centurion's faith and reasoning, spoke the word, and the slave was healed (verses 9-10).

John's gospel is helpfully illuminated by this concept of brokerage. Jesus is the Word that was with God in the beginning (1:1), became flesh (1:14), brought the fullness of God's grace, truth, and glory to humankind (1:17), and revealed God (1:18). In him the fullness of God's spirit is ever present (3:34), therefore he speaks the words of God and mediates eternal life to those who obey him (3:36). He provides access to living water (4:11) and reveals all there is to know about God (4:25). As God's son he is to be honored as the Father's agent, the one who imitates what he sees the Father doing, one who possesses within himself the power of life and death (5:19-26). He is the bread of life (6:35), the light of the world (8:12), the gate for the sheep (10:7), and the good shepherd (10:11). He is one with the Father (10:30) and the resurrection and the life (11:25). He is the way, the truth, and the life (14:6) and as one is instructed to have faith in God so one is instructed to have faith in Jesus (14:1). As God's broker, clients may address him as if he were their patron (20:28). Throughout John's gospel there is little mention of the role or function of the spirit until talk of Jesus' departure. It is at this juncture that the spirit appears to assume or take over the role of brokerage that Jesus is presented exercising throughout the gospel. But the presentation of the spirit as "another paraclete" (14:16), or as a "replacement broker" (14:26; 16:13-15), is not without its problems.

In the Gospel of John, the word "spirit" (Greek, pneuma) occurs 24 times. In the Farewell Discourse, pneuma occurs 4 times, once preceded by the adjective holy (Greek, hagion). If 14:26 is reliable, then the Holy Spirit is equated with the figure of the Paraclete.[13] But the real problem is found when one compares the usage of pneuma in John before and after its usage in the Farewell Discourse.

In the Farewell Discourse, it seems apparent that the Paraclete/pneuma is either a real person, distinct from the Father and Son, or is presented "as if" a person by means of a literary or rhetorical personification. Consider the following activities or functions of the Paraclete: being sent, proceeding, and testifying (14:26); reproving (14:8); guiding, speaking, prophesying (16:13); and glorifying and revealing (16:14). These are all the activities or functions of a person. Whereas (some) Trinitarian interpreters see this as clear support for their doctrine, Unitarians and Binitarians object. Here's why.

Both before and after the Farewell Discourse the pneuma is presented along the lines of traditional Jewish or OT understandings of the spirit (Usage 2 in my Introduction). The spirit is simply God's (the Father's) active but impersonal power and presence. This will become clear in a moment when I comment on some select passages. What seems to have taken place in the Farewell Discourse is that the empowerment so often associated with the spirit (testifying, reproving, guiding, speaking, revealing) and manifested *through* human agents, is presented in the abstract as if this empowerment was located in a spiritual being other than the Father and/or the Son. Hence the literary device of personification. I will argue that the enigmatic presentation of the spirit in 7:37-39 provides one key to this development. The concept of brokerage provides another. But, in order to make my line of argument clear, I need to first comment on a few select passages.

Prior to the Farewell Discourse, the spirit is said to have descended upon Jesus at his baptism as testified to by John the Baptist (1:32-33) giving John the Baptist the insight that Jesus was the one who would baptize others in holy spirit. From a Jewish perspective, this coheres with the prophecies of Joel (3:1-5), Isaiah (42:1), Jeremiah (31:31-34) and Ezekiel (36:25-27), all of which speak of a future time when God would empower his people with the gift of his spirit, his power and presence. There is no need to postulate, against this background, any notion of a third person or an independent being called the Spirit. In 3:34, Jesus' possession of the fullness of spirit is what guarantees the truth of his teaching. There is neither need nor hint of the notion of an additional "third person."

Prior to the Farewell Discourse, Jesus instructs Nicodemus about being born of the Spirit (3:1-7). Here, in my judgment, the Spirit refers to God the Father as a synonym or metonym (Usage 1 in my Introduction). This seems justified by the clear statement in 4:24 that God (the Father, see verse 23) is Spirit. Both contexts (3:1-7 and 4:20-24) make it clear that a contrast is being made between the realm of humankind (physical birth/worship in Gerizim vs Jerusalem)) and the realm of God (the spiritual).

After the Farewell Discourse, pneuma is used twice. Both are significant and informative. In 19:30, Jesus "bows his head" and "hands over the spirit" (Greek: klinas ten kephalen and paredoken to pneuma). On one level, the physical, Jesus is presented as simply dying. He bows his head and quits breathing. On another level, the spiritual, Jesus is presented as finishing the task the Father had called him to (19:30 also presents Jesus as crying "it is finished"). Jesus dies, completes his mission, and is now in a position to mediate the promised spirit (spoken of in the above OT prophecies) to his followers. There is no need here to conceive of this spirit as a third person, even though the promise of this spirit was personified as the Paraclete in the Farewell Discourse. 20:22 presents pretty much the same reality as 19:30, although in a different setting. In 20:22, Jesus appears to his disciples in his resurrected state, commissions them (verse 21), and then breathes upon them with the command to receive holy spirit (Greek: labete pneuma hagion). It seems clear from the context that Jesus is equipping them with the spiritual enablement that they will need in order to carry on their task of ministry. Again, Usage 2, the traditional OT understanding of the spirit as divine enablement, seems sufficient. A Trinitarian understanding adds nothing to the sense here, but confusion.

What I am attempting to demonstrate is the inconsistency in John between the pre and post Farewell Discourse impersonal (Usage 2) presentation of the spirit and the personal (or personification) presentation of the Spirit as Paraclete in the Farewell Discourse. How do I account for this inconsistency and continue to argue the Binitarian position? As stated above, I see the presentation of the spirit in 7:37-39 and the concept of brokerage as critical.

In 7:37-39, Jesus presents himself, on the last day of the feast of Tabernacles, as the source of living water. His public proclamation receives this qualification (or narrator's aside): "He said this in reference to the Spirit that those who came to believe in him were to receive" (*NAB*). A further note is then added: "There was, of course, no Spirit yet, because Jesus had not yet been glorified" (*NAB*). On the face of things, this stands in contradiction to the clear assertions of the spirit's presence and activity in 1:32-33, 3:5-8, 34, 4:23-24, 6:63, and even 14:17. Stepping outside of the Gospel of John for a moment, in order to statistically strengthen my point, the spirit seems clearly present in the lives of Jesus' followers, prior to his death and resurrection, in the following passages: Matthew 10:1, 20; Mark 6:13; 13:11; Luke 1:15, 17, 41, 67; 2:25-27, 38; and 11:13. How should this apparent discrepancy be explained?

It seems that the best remedy would be to suggest that John's statement, "There was. . .no Spirit yet" (7:39: Greek, oupo gar ayn pneuma), was simply vague and unfortunate. The evangelists, writers like the rest of us, often leave some of their thoughts vague or unclear. Clarity might be provided if the evangelist had stated something like this: "Although spiritual enablement is now available, it is nothing like what it will be after Jesus completes his mission." John, like the rest of the NT authors, labored under the burden of, on the one hand, demonstrating continuity with OT concepts (like holy spirit), and on the other, demonstrating that something new, improved, final, and definitive had arrived. Several translators (*AMP, KJV, DR, NASB, and NIV*) add the word "given" after "yet" in an attempt to provide some clarity.[14] John himself, in the Farewell Discourse (14:17), seems aware of his inconsistency when he has Jesus make a distinction between the spirit's presence "with" (Greek, para) them now (in a pre-cross and resurrection state) and the spirit's future presence "in" (Greek, en) them after the cross and the resurrection. I suggest that, laboring under this distinction of pre and post cross/resurrection understandings of the spirit, the evangelist fumbled some passages (7:37-39 and 14:17) and resorted to personification for the others (the Farewell Discourse). The concept of brokerage reinforces this need for personification.

In NT thought, Jesus is the final and definitive broker of God's blessings (recall Hebrews 1:1-2). This is stressed throughout the Gospel of John as already pointed out. In order to stress this point, it seems to me, the author of the Gospel of John transferred Jesus' functions as God's broker to the Spirit/Paraclete necessitating the Spirit's personification. What Jesus used to do as God's broker, the Spirit now does. Just as Jesus was sent by the Father (3:17), so the Paraclete is sent by Jesus and the Father (14:16 and 26). Just as Jesus reveals the Father (14:9), so the Paraclete will teach the believers all things (14:26). Just as Jesus abode with the disciples and is now in the disciples (14:20), so the Paraclete abides in the disciples (14:17). Just as Jesus convicts the world concerning sin (9:39-41), so does the Paraclete (16:8-11). Just as Jesus is the Truth (14:6), so the Paraclete is the Spirit of Truth (14:17). Other parallels could be mentioned, but the point seems to be that the concept of a personified Paraclete was the Evangelist's way of preserving his message that Jesus was the final and definitive revelation of God. The concept of the Paraclete, in light of the other teaching about the spirit in John (and the rest of the NT and OT for that matter), seems best understood as a metaphor for revelation. It was a way of talking about and preserving the central NT insight that in Jesus, and only in Jesus, God is fully and finally revealed. This impelled the author of the Gospel of John to resort to the device of personification, a device commonly utilized when one is attempting to communicate difficult concepts.[15] The idea that Jesus *remains* the final and full revelation of God even in light of his *absence* is a difficult concept. The Paraclete concept allows this sole revelation of God to continue. One might develop this concept in a Trinity direction (as we will see in the next chapter) but Binitarians stop short of this development insisting on the mere personification of the Paraclete figure rather than on the need for the creation of a new hypostasis within the Godhead. It does seem the simpler option. The Paraclete thus considered becomes a metaphor for God's continued revelation through Christ. This conclusion coheres with the Binitarian direction of the rest of the NT and provides a reasonable explanation for the fourth gospel's inconsistent presentation of the spirit, impersonal before and after the Farewell Discourse, personal within the Discourse. The model of brokerage facilitates the personification. In addition to these arguments, one might appeal to precedents in Jewish tradition whereby the transfer of someone's spirit to a successor resulted in similar hyperbole. For example, Elisha receives a double portion of the spirit of Elijah (2 Kings 2:9-15) and both Jesus (Mark 6:15) and John the Baptist (Matthew 11:14 and John 1:21) are thought themselves to be Elijah.

More could be said to defend the Binitarian position. But this seems like a good point to conclude. The next chapter on Trinitarianism will pick up where this chapter has left off, focusing upon interpretations of the spirit but developing them in a different direction.

Notes

1. Among the key Binitarian passages are the following: Matthew 11:27; 23:9-10; Mark 13:32; John 1:1, 18; 5:23, 26; 8:14-19, 29; 10:15, 30; 14:1, 6, 10; 15:1; 20:22; Romans 1:7; 16:27; 1 Corinthians 1:3; 15:28; 2 Corinthians 1:2; Ephesians 1:2; 6:23; Philippians 1:2; Colossians 1:2; 1 Thessalonians 1:3; 2 Thessalonians 1:2; 1 Timothy 1:2; 2:5; 2 Timothy 1:2; Titus 1:4; Philemon 3; Hebrew 1:1-2; 13:20-21; James 1:1; 1 Peter 1:3; 5:10; 2 Peter 1:1-2; 1 John 1:3; 5:1; 2 John 1:3; Jude 1; and Revelation 5:13. Among the key Trinitarian passages are the following: Matthew 28:19; John 16:13; 1 Corinthians 12:4-6; 2 Corinthians 13:14; Ephesians 4:6; Hebrews 9:14; 1 Peter 1:2; and 1 John 4:13-14.
2. J. T. Forestell, "Proverbs," in *The Jerome Biblical Commentary*. R. E. Brown, J. A. Fitzmeyer & R. E. Murphy, editors, (Englewood Cliffs: Prentice Hall, 1968), points out that although qanah has to do with "acquisition by way of birth" and therefore may suggest "creation," it also could be understood in terms of "generation," and could be understood in the sense of the "eternal generation" spoken of in Trinitarian (or Binitarian) theology. Forestell points out that the author of Proverbs is "trying to assert, in the best way he can, the absolute priority of Wisdom and her origin from God before all creation,"

500. James Strong, editor, *The Exhaustive Concordance of the Bible* (Nashville: Abingdon, 1979), 104, lists the following as possible translations of qanah: to erect; create; procure; purchase; attain; and buy. See also Francis Brown, S. R. Driver, and Charles A. Briggs. *A Hebrew and English Lexicon of the Old Testament*, rev. ed. (Oxford: Clarendon, 1972), 888 and 651, for the range of meanings of these terms. Origen, in his discussion of the generation of the Son and the procession of the Spirit, interprets the corresponding Greek terms (genetos and ktizein) for the Hebrew qanah in a metaphorical rather than in a literal manner. See David W. Bercot, *A Dictionary of Christian Beliefs* (Peabody: Hendrickson, 1998), 280.

3. For discussion and documentation see J. B. Lightfoot, *Saint Paul's Epistles to the Colossians and to Philemon* (Grand Rapids: Zondervan, 1976, reprint of revised 1879 edition), 146-47.

4. The four variants are: The unique one (ho monogenes); the unique son (ho monogenes huios); the unique God (ho monogenes theos); and unique God (monogenes theos). A thorough discussion of the scholarly preferences and the implications for understanding the deity of Jesus may be found in Murray J. Harris, *Jesus as God: The New Testament Use of Theos in Reference to Jesus* (Grand Rapids: Baker, 1992), 73-103.

5. H. E. Dana & Julius Mantey, *A Manual Grammar of the Greek New Testament* (Toronto: MacMillan, 1955), 193, state: "The aorist signifies nothing as to completeness, but simply presents the action as attained. It states the fact of the action or event without regard to its *duration*" (italics original). Hence, when the aorist is used in a comparative or contrastive manner, as here in Hebrews 1:1-2, completeness or finality may be inferred.

6. See Larry E. Hurtado, *At the Origins of Christian Worship: The Context and Character of Earliest Christian Devotion* (Grand Rapids: Eerdmans, 1999), 63-97, for detailed comments.

7. Cf. 1 Corinthians 14:26; Colossians 3:16-17; Ephesians 5:18-20; James 5:14; Acts 16:25; Philippians 2:6-11; Colossians 1:15-20; John 1:1-18; Ephesians 5:14; and 1 Timothy 3:16. Pliny, the late first century governor of Bithynia, is often cited for support of the alleged practice of Christians singing hymns to Christ "as a god." Aloys Grillmeyer, (translated by J. S. Bowden), *Christ in Christian Tradition: From the Apostolic Age to Chalcedon* (New York: Sheed and Ward, 1965.), 101-102, provides not only the Latin text of Pliny's comment, but adds evidence from several apocryphal Christian texts that give further support to the early Christian practice of addressing prayers and praise to Jesus.

8. The classic exposition of the two powers "heresy" is found in A. F. Segal, *Two Powers in Heaven: Early Rabbinic Reports about Christianity and Gnosticism* (Leiden: Brill, 1977). Typical of the early focus upon "two gods" is the following: "Origen said: 'Do we acknowledge two Gods?' Heraclides said: ' Yes; the power is one.' Origen said: 'But since our brethren are shocked by the affirmation that there are two Gods, the subject must be examined with care in order to show in what respect they are two and in what respect the two are one God.'" Cited in Robert M. Grant, *The Early Christian Doctrine of God* (Charlottesville: University Press of Virginia, 1966), 70.

9. See George Montague, *The Holy Spirit: The Growth of a Biblical Tradition: A Commentary on the Principal Texts of the Old and New Testaments* (New York: Paulist, 1976), 359. Montague states: "If we seem to have reached a point of confusion, in which we do not know whether the Holy Spirit is really a distinct person or whether he is in reality the presence and activity of the Father and the Son, it means that we have reached the summit of New Testament pneumatology...The Paraclete is a living, personal presence given by the Father and Jesus glorified to supply for Jesus' physical absence until

his return. The Spirit is both a person and the personal, spiritual presence of the Father and the Son. That is where the mystery lies." Binitarians would argue for the "spiritual presence," not the "person."

10. The Farewell Discourse occupies Chapters 14-17. It plausibly was composed at a late stage in the development of the Gospel of John. See Urban C. VonWahlde, *The Earliest Version of John's Gospel: Recovering the Gospel of Signs* (Wilmington: Michael Glazier, 1989), 178-82. VonWahlde argues that the 2nd edition of the gospel shifted the underlying principle of faith from signs to the activity of the Spirit.

11. See G. Braumann, "Advocate, Paraclete, Helper," in *The New International Dictionary of New Testament Theology, Volume 1* (Grand Rapids: Zondervan, 1975), 88-91.

12. Patricia Gates Brown has written an entire monograph interpreting the concept of Spirit in the Gospel and First Epistle of John in light of this model, *Spirit in the Writings of John: Johannine Pneumatology in Social-Science Perspective* (London: T & T Clark, 2003).

13. Based on a few minor variant readings, some scholars speculate that the original of 14:26 was without the explicit identification of the Paraclete as the Holy Spirit. Yet, in the 4 occurrences of the Paraclete (14:26; 15:26; 16:7; and 16:13) the identification of the Paraclete with the [Holy] Spirit seems natural, although implicit. Cf. R. E. Brown, *The Gospel According to John, Volume 2* (Garden City: Doubleday, 1966), 650-51.

14. There is some manuscript support for this addition but it seems unlikely that it represents the original. See S. H. Hooker, "The Spirit Was Not Yet," Pp. 372-80 in *New Testament Studies* 9, 1962, especially, 372.

15. A pertinent and related difficult concept is that of the tension between God's transcendence and immanence. In the OT (and NT) this is resolved by the concept of spirit. God himself stays in heaven (the transcendent realm) whereas the spirit is active upon earth (the immanent realm). But in order to give life, animation, and relevance the spirit's activity at times was personified, as in the case of wisdom, at times was hypostatized, as in the case of the angel of the Lord. Against this background, the personification of the spirit in terms of the Paraclete figure is more understandable. Helmer Ringgren's doctoral thesis on this is quite helpful: *Word and Wisdom: Studies in the Hypostatization of Divine Qualities and Functions* (Lund: H Ohlsson's boktr, 1947).

Chapter Four
The Trinitarian Model

As with the previous models, I begin with a brief summary of the Trinitarian position. An expansion of the arguments and exegesis of key texts then follows.

A Brief Summary of the Trinitarian Position

A careful and prayerful reflection on the scriptural and traditional data regarding Father, Son, and Spirit consistently and constantly leads to the affirmation of a triune understanding of the Godhead, namely, that God is one in substance, three in persons. Some Trinitarians maintain that the Trinity is clearly taught in the NT (fundamentalists, conservative evangelicals, and some conservative mainline denominations), whereas others stress that the dogma of the Trinity is present only in seed form or implicitly (liberal theologians and most mainline denominations). This "in house" division represents two differing apologetics for the doctrine of the Trinity. The former appeals to scripture alone. The latter appeals to both scripture and tradition, depending more heavily upon notions of progressive revelation and the development of dogma.

Scripture frequently presents the Spirit as a person, distinct from Father and Son, and in categories that would demand or at least suggest its deification. Scripture is also equally clear regarding the affirmation that there is only one God. The developments of the ongoing tradition confirm these insights by the teachings of several early Christian theologians (Tertullian; Irenaeus; Origen; Athanasius; Basil; Gregory of Nazianzus; Gregory of Nyssa; Hilary; Augustine) and finally by the Councils of Nicea (325 CE), Constantinople (381 CE), and Chalcedon (451 CE). Furthermore, Trinitarianism seems demanded in any presupposition of Binitarianism. Once one grants that there are two persons in the Godhead (as in Father and Son), a principle of union for these two is demanded. The only adequate principle of union would be something which itself was divine in the fullest sense of the term. As argued in the previous chapter on Binitarianism, only God can reveal God. If the Holy Spirit's task is to reveal Christ, who in turn reveals the Father, then the Holy Spirit must be adequate to the task.

This last thought receives additional force when it is united with the reasoning set forth in the chapter on Binitarianism on the implications for Jesus' deity derived from the notions of Jesus' death as a ransom and expiation/propitiation for the sins of the world. Trinitarians support the Binitarian reasoning here but reinforce it with implications regarding the necessity of the Spirit's deity in making the redemptive significance of the death of Jesus effective and real in the life of the individual, the liturgy of the church, and its proclamation to the world. God has two hands through which he accomplishes his revelation and salvation of the world, the Word (Jesus) and the Spirit.

Furthermore, a Trinitarian understanding of God not only does justice to the overall sense of scripture, tradition, and individual and ecclesial religious experience, it also satisfies the demands of deep philosophical reflection. If God is love, and if that love is eternal, only a Trinitarian understanding of God allows that love to truly exists as love. Love, by nature, is reciprocal. Traditional monotheism, with its insistence on one person, does not allow the static singularity and simplicity of God to incorporate any reciprocal love. A Trinitarian notion of God allows God to love and to be loved and that eternally and blissfully.

Finally, and also philosophically, a Trinitarian view of God allows one to envision creation as a free act, rather than as a necessity. God, as an interrelated society of persons existing in reciprocal love, has neither lack nor need. Creation, therefore, is a free gift. The eternally satisfied and satisfying divine love calls forth and calls to itself all creatures.

An Expansion of the Above Arguments

The Spirit as a distinct divine Person

There is no question that the Spirit is distinct from the Father and the Son. Too many biblical passages would be obscured if this were not the case.[1] What is problematic, is that the Spirit is a bona fide person and a divine one at that! In this section, I will argue for the person issue. In a later section, I will argue for the divine issue. But first a word about the concept of a person.

The chief characteristics of a human person are: self-awareness; volition; capacity for relationship; and, inherent dignity.[2] Since religious human beings worship God, God must at least possess these characteristics; otherwise human beings find themselves worshipping something inferior. But all talk about God is anthropomorphic and analogical. In order for human beings to worship God, God must at least be personal in some sense analogous to human personhood. But God's personhood certainly could be different and of a different order than human personhood. In Trinitarian thought, the Father, Son, and Spirit are distinct persons (the earlier terms were the Latin prosopon and the Greek hypostasis; the middles ages introduced the Latin term existentia; and moderns have suggested the English term "modes").[3] But whatever the terms used, and no new term appears more suitable than person, one needs to understand that the persons of the Trinity are persons in a sense much different than human persons. The word mystery comes to mind as an adjective for divine persons.

In Trinitarian thought, the Father is not the Son, and the Son is not the Spirit, and the Spirit preserves distinction from both Father and Son. The Father is unbegotten, the Son is generated, and the Spirit is spirated. There is distinction within unity. There is a unique interrelationship among these persons that together constitutes the one God (understood here not as person but as substance). The distinction of the persons in the Godhead is unlike the distinction of persons within human society, thus creating some of the understandable confusion in trying to understand the Trinity. When human beings conceive of a person, they automatically conceive of that person as existing separately from any other person. Yet all human beings share the same nature (humanity).[4] Likewise, the three divine persons share the one nature (God). Yet, the distinction among the persons is only analogous to the distinction among separate human persons.

Unitarians and Binitarians, as argued in the previous two chapters, offer alternative explanations for the apparent personhood of the Spirit. Essentially, personification is offered as the preferred explanation. Although some Trinitarian advocates would want to argue over the exegetical details and decisions regarding to personify or to not personify, I prefer to concede. Let the Unitarians and Binitarians be correct about each and every individual passage deemed better understood as a personification of the Spirit. It's not any individual passage per se that justifies the doctrine of the Trinity; it's the collective sense and drift of scripture, tradition, and ecclesial religious experience. The Trinity is not really affirmed by scripture. Rather, it is intimated. The NT merely hints at the Trinity. The NT is neither dogmatic nor systematic. Nevertheless, the instincts and impulses of a Trinitarian conception of God seem present.

Earlier I quoted the Catholic Catechism regarding the moment of the revelation of the doctrine of the Trinity (see page 35 and note 21 in Chapter Two). The Trinity, said to be revealed at Pentecost, was not revealed in so many words (after all, the word "trinity" was not coined until Tertullian invented it in 192 CE). Rather, the revelation of the Trinity was set in motion at Pentecost. It took four centuries to unpack it and clarify it. Its unpacking and clarification continue to the present moment and will (rightfully) continue throughout all eternity. God should be allowed to retain the rights to remain a mystery! Trinitarians who argue with Unitarians and Binitarians over the particular details of this, that, or the other scripture often miss the point I am attempting to make here. Trinitarian Christians, wrongly I suggest, are often taught to read their doctrine back into scripture as if it was patently or blatantly there. No wonder no one likes to discuss the scriptures on this topic! Way too much heat, way too little light! I will continue to argue for the plausibility of the Trinity, but not upon a naïve literal or propositional approach to scripture. Rather, I will appeal to the hermeneutics of progressive revelation, the sensus plenior, and the need for the development of dogma. The key underlying, although admittedly abstract, interpretive principles are: only God can reveal God; two persons allowed into the Godhead demand a third; God is eternal reciprocal love; and creation is truly a free gift.

So, is the Spirit a person? Yes. And as mentioned, I do not base this upon the exegesis of any particular scripture. Rather, one might initially ask: Why do we see a progressive or disproportionate personification of the Spirit in the NT? It does seem that some writings of the NT (Luke-Acts; Paul; John) engage more excessively in the personification of the Spirit than do other writings (Mark; James; 1-2 Peter). Perhaps there was more to it than mere personification. At least the later Church thought so. Many Christians today continue to think this way. Here are some justifications.

The Spirit as the New and Effective Revealer of God

In the OT, the spirit of God was a way of speaking about God in his immanent activities. It was best understood as either a synonym/metonym for God or as an impersonal gift of power. In the NT, however, something changed. The initial burst of revelation that launched Christianity was the cross-resurrection-Pentecost event. This clearly produced an unprecedented development of ideas. Jesus was now experienced as truly alive in a transformed state. Jesus was experienced as "Lord," commissioning and empowering his followers as never before. This revelation not only generated a Binitarian mutation within Jewish monotheism but also a Trinitarian mutation. The NT authors labored under old conceptions as they struggled to articulate the new revelation. Like new wine, the new revelation could no longer be contained in old wineskins (cf. Mark 2:21-22). Lower case spirit would no longer suffice. An upper case Spirit was required. Some NT authors retained the old conception of spirit, others pushed in a new direction. The excessive and poignant personification of the Spirit was how they pushed. It was left for the later church to state clearly and explicitly the new revelation that the NT authors were struggling to announce and perhaps could only hint at (review my comments on Hebrews 1:1-2 on pages 40-42, John 7:37-39 on pages 46-47, and John 19:30 on page 46).[5]

The deification of the Spirit, in part, mirrors the process by which the Son was deified. In light of the cross-resurrection-Pentecost event, Christians began to ransack all prior OT categories of theological understanding that would help them articulate how they were experiencing and understanding Jesus. Two primary categories that were applied to Jesus were word and wisdom. Jesus was understood as the pre-existent word and wisdom of God. Word and wisdom were simply attributes or functions of Yahweh that eventually became personified.[6] When these categories were applied to Jesus, word and wisdom then made a shift from personification to hypostatization.[7] Since Jesus was an actual person, and portrayed as pre-existent word and wisdom (see especially John 1:1-5; 8:58; and 17:5), then, by this process, the OT personified word and wisdom actually "become" the pre-incarnate person of Jesus. Applying this principle or logic to the Spirit lends itself to understanding how the Spirit could undergo a similar process, making the transition from personification to hypostatization. The justification for elevating the Spirit from a mere personification of Yahweh's activities to an actual distinct hypostasis or person is found not in the exegesis of any particular text but in the entire complex of the drift of scripture, tradition, individual and ecclesial religious experience, Christological parallels, and underlying philosophical considerations. Although explaining the concept of the Trinity is impossible, explaining the process by which it developed isn't. Hopefully, some of the suggestions I am making here are helping the reader to at least conceive or imagine why the concept of the Trinity emerged out of the tumult of the first few centuries of Christianity, particularly the dynamic of its (at least Binitarian) Christological commitment.

The Spirit and Religious Experience

Religious experience, then, just as much as scripture and tradition, forms part of the platform for the doctrine of the Trinity. Agreed, the NT is neither clear nor explicit regarding the Trinity, at least at the level of so many clear statements. But religious experience often generates new beliefs as well as legitimizing prior beliefs.[8] For example, prior to Paul's "mystery" revelation (see Ephesians 3:1-6) all converts to Christianity first had to become Jews (cf. Acts 15:1). Paul's revelation appears to flatly contradict Genesis 17:7 where circumcision is presented as an everlasting covenant (it is interesting that Paul never cites or mentions Genesis 17 in any of his writings). By analogy, the shift from impersonal notions of the spirit to personal notions finds suggestive warrant. Christians might ask themselves just how they "know" God, that Jesus is Lord, and that God loves them. The NT seems quite clear that this knowledge is the result of the gift of the Spirit (see Romans 5:5; 8:9; 1 Corinthians 12:3; Galatians 4:6 and 1 John 3:24). If the Spirit is that which makes Christ real to Christians, and therefore God real to Christians, that might give Christians pause to consider just who or what the Spirit is. True, the NT pattern was to worship God through Jesus in the power of the Spirit. But, as argued in the chapter on Binitarianism, although God is the object of worship, Christ is the content. The Spirit is the medium by which all this is comprehended. Consider this: As Christians worship God the Father, they do so knowing that the only basis they have for access to God's presence is the blood of Christ (Ephesians 2:13). As one worships God, does all adoration and thanksgiving and love direct itself solely to the Father? What role does Christ play in Christian worship? Does one thank Jesus, set him aside, and then spend "time" in adoration of God? How does one separate the Son and the Father in the act of worship? Is it 90% devotion for the Father and 10% for the Son? Binitarians and Trinitarians answer that it is 100% to each as together they constitute the One God. Furthermore, from a Trinitarian perspective, access would be denied without the Spirit (Ephesians 2:18). It is the Spirit that makes the Christian revelation effective and alive in the experience of the believer. This, among other considerations, has caused the majority of Christians to affirm the deity of the Spirit. Christians delight in the Triune God. The Father is author of salvation, the Son is agent, the Spirit actualizes and guarantees the whole thing. The Spirit is God in us, the Son is God for us, and the Father is God above us. Since God and Jesus reside now in heaven, it is only with the reality and deity of the Spirit that Christians make claim to a unique and definitive experience of God.

The Spirit as the Principle of Union

The previous argument regarding the Spirit and religious experience is probably only persuasive for those already predisposed to experience or encounter God in a Trinitarian sense. Hence, I conclude my thoughts on the Trinitarian model with one last attempt to appeal to reason, or at least to a reason, for giving the Trinity further consideration.

Plato notes in his *Timaeus*: "two things alone cannot be satisfactorily united without a third; for there must be some bond between them drawing them together."[9] In context, Plato is discussing geometry, the notion of the geometric mean, where A is to B in exactly the same ratio as B is to C. Applied to the Trinity, what Christ is to God the Father (the revealer), the Spirit is to Christ (the revealer). Furthermore, Augustine is famous for defining the Spirit as the bond of love between the Father and the Son. If the Father is distinct from the Son, and the Son distinct from the Father, yet both God (eternal and reciprocal love), then the bond which unites, love itself, must also be distinct. Distinct yes. Separate no. Three persons, one God.

Reality comes in threes. Three is the number of wholeness and fullness. A family consists of father-mother-child. Time consists of past, present, and future. Experience is measured by anticipation-realization-memory. Consciousness distinguishes being from knowing and willing. Matter is liquid, solid, or gas. The atom is made up of electron, neutron, and proton. Grammar knows of three voices, three persons, and three degrees of comparison. In ethics, that which is right is the mean between the extremes. Other examples could be triplicated. The point here is that the doctrine of the Trinity has clear mathematical, conceptual, and experiential appeal.[10]

So much more could be and should be said with regard to the merits of the Trinitarian conception of God. Others, much more qualified than myself, and addressing the topic from a different angles, should be consulted.[11] Hopefully, this chapter will suffice as an introductory argument for translating the Holy

Spirit with all the rights and privileges that pertain to one who is distinct from the Father and the Son but at the same time coequal as personal deity.

Notes

1. The following are clear passages making such a distinction: Matthew 28:18-20; John 14:16, 26; 15:26; 16:7; Acts 13:2; 15:28; Romans 8:16; 2 Corinthians 13:14; Galatians 3:1-5 with 4:6; Ephesians 1:13; 4:4-6, 30; Hebrews 9:14 and Revelation 22:17. Nevertheless, passages such as 1 Corinthians 2:10-16 (discussed above pages 8-11) and 2 Corinthians 3:17 "Now the Lord is the Spirit" (*NAB*), appear problematic.
2. According to Donald Gelpi, *The Divine Mother: A Trinitarian Theology of the Holy Spirit* (Lanham: University Press of America, 1984), 108, Boethius defined person as "the individual substance of a rational nature."
3. See Gelpi, *ibid*, 103-124.
4. This statement raises the perplexing issue of how Jesus can be both human (one of us) and God (one of them). Further complicating Trinitarian discussion, but deemed beyond the scope or depth of the treatment here, is the perplexing question of how Jesus' human "person" can be the same as his divine "person." It is easy to understand Jesus, as one of us, as a human person. It is difficult to understand that, although one of us, he really is different!
5. Since Nicea was so focused on the proper relation between the Son and the Father, all it declared with regard to the Holy Spirit was: "and [we believe] in the Holy Spirit." The Council at Constantinople in 381 CE provided greater clarity: ""And in the Holy Spirit, the Lord and life-giver, Who proceeds from the Father, Who is worshiped and glorified together with the Father and the Son." Cited from Rebecca Moore, *Voices of Christianity: A Global Introduction* (Boston: McGraw Hill, 2006), 90.
6. See Isaiah 55:1-11, especially verse 11 for the personification of the word. See Proverbs 8, the entire chapter, for an example of the personification of wisdom.
7. Illustration Five (page 72) makes an attempt to depict this process. A conceptual problem arises when one notes that Word and Wisdom are often synonymous and interchangeable (as seen, for example, when comparing Sirach 42:15 and/or Wisdom 9:1 with Psalm 136:12 and/or Jeremiah 10:12). If they were interchangeable and synonymous in the OT, how can they be distinguished in the NT, or the post NT era to be more precise? For example, Irenaeus states: "I have also largely demonstrated that the Word, namely the Son, was always with the Father. And that Wisdom also, who is the Spirit, was present with Him before all creation," cited in David Bercot, editor, *A Dictionary of Christian Beliefs* (Peabody: Hendrickson, 1998), 343. Answer: the demands of my central hermeneutical principles (presented in this Chapter) override previous conceptions. What were mere personifications of God's presence and work in the world have become, by reason of the Incarnation and corresponding interpretive principles, two distinct hypostases.
8. This is argued for and illustrated by Larry Hurtado, *How on Earth Did Jesus Become God? Historical Questions about Earliest Devotion to Jesus* (Grand Rapids: Eerdmans, 2005), 179-204.
9. Cited from David Fideler, *Jesus Christ Sun of God: Ancient Cosmology and Early Christian Symbolism* (Wheaton: Quest Books, 1993), 69.

58   Chapter Four

10. Christianity is not the only religion to conceptualize divine reality as co-existing in three separate modes. Consider this quote from Alain Danielou, *Yoga* (Rochester: Inner Traditions International, 1991), 14: "Everything that exists can be reduced to a balance of forces creating substance; a centripetal, concentrating force called Vishnu; a centrifugal dispersive force called Shiva; and a resulting giving birth to the circular movement of the stars and atoms, or matter, called Brahman." Thus the Hindu creator, sustainer, and destroyer conception of God.

11. R. P. C. Hanson's, *The Search for the Christian Doctrine of God* (Edinburgh: T & T Clark, 1988) nearly 1,000 pages, would provide the interested reader with many fascinating details concerning the evolution of the doctrine of the Trinity.

Chapter Five
The Non-Sectarian Model

My presentation of the Non-Sectarian Model follows suit with the previous models. I begin with a brief overview of the model, follow with an elaboration of its arguments, and reflect back upon the exegesis of key passages.

A Brief Summary of the Non-Sectarian Position

The Non-Sectarian position, while respecting the reasonableness of several of the arguments put forth by Unitarians, Binitarians, and Trinitarians, nevertheless, rejects the ultimate cogency of any of the previous views. Analogous to a math problem involving the division of an uneven number by an even number, there is always a remainder such that the solution to the problem is not even and tidy. One may invoke the preponderance of the evidence, or the category of mystery, but one may also simply conclude that, to date, none of the models are satisfactory. This model, therefore, identifies the weaknesses and inconsistencies in each of the models.

The Non-Sectarian position is pragmatically and ecumenically oriented. Unitarianism, Binitarianism, and Trinitarianism are paradigms of convenience, ways of talking about God according to established traditions of liturgy and confession. They are useful in that they allow adherents to image, understand, and worship God. Although a true and correct view of God is important, the truth is that this "true and correct" view remains obscured. Christians should agree to disagree and tolerate one anothers' models, seeking as much common ground as possible. May I suggest here the Sermon on the Mount (Matthew 5-8)? The "correct" view seems out of reach. To date, no one has argued so convincingly that a significant movement or exodus of believers from one camp to the other has occurred. True, the Trinitarian camp is considered mainstream, but that could be a result of having attained political power and engaged in censorship and suppression of opposing views.[1]

Chapter Five

An Expansion of the Above Arguments

Unitarianism

The Unitarian position finds its strength in its rational and logical consistency, at least in terms of the plain, literal, and surface meaning of scripture. Unitarianism adheres to the principle that the clear verse interprets the obscure verse. A case was made in Chapter Two (the Unitarian chapter) that the scripture is unanimous and clear that there is one God, the Father. Passages that seem to present the Son and/or the Spirit as deity are subordinate to alternative and, admittedly, in many cases, more plausible interpretations. Thus a harmony is achieved. But this strength of Unitarianism turns out also to be its weakness.

The Bible is not merely a rational, logical, systematic, coherent, and consistent body of information. Yes, it does provide some basis for the exercise of the above adjectives, but the Bible gives witness to generations of believers who challenged previously held views. There does seem to be room for the notion of progressive revelation, innovations, and even radical revolutions in thinking. Several tensions exist in the canon of scripture.

Is the human soul mortal (Genesis 3:22; Ecclesiastes 9:5; 1 Timothy 6:16) or immortal (Mark 9:4; John 14:3; 2 Corinthians 5:1-2; Philippians 1:21-23; Revelation 6:9)? Does law trump grace (Matthew 7:21-23; James 2:8 and 18; Hebrews 10:26-31; 1 Peter 4:17-18) or does grace trump law (John 5:24; Romans 3:27-28; Ephesians 2:8)? Is prosperity in life based on righteous living (Psalms and Proverbs) or is life basically chaotic and unfair (Job and Ecclesiastes)? Is God more interested in ritual, doctrine, and inner group cohesion (Leviticus; Deuteronomy; 1 John) or is God more interested in social justice (the Prophets)? Should the church be organized under the authority of a central God appointed leader (Moses; Peter), or elders, or bishops, or charismatic individuals, or the mutual consent of the laity? Tensions abound and revelations change with the demands, needs, interests, and circumstances of the times. God's revelation may be "in the book" (Bible) but it also seems to reside in the communities that preserve the teachings of the book. Interpretation is dynamic not static. Theologians, trained not just in rote scripture, but also in philosophy and rhetoric, often are able to mine scripture, and individual and ecclesial experience, to "see" what might lie deeper within the reservoirs of revelation. Thus, Binitarians and Trinitarians, "see" the deity of Jesus. Scripture, the nature of the events of scripture (cross-resurrection-gift of spirit), underlying philosophical principles (the inner logic of atonement; only God reveal God; progressive revelation), the character of liturgical practices (prayer; confessions; creeds; baptism; hymns), all merge together and carry believers to a conclusion other than Unitarianism.

Certainly, few Unitarians will be persuaded by these objections. But these objections do cry out for response. The Unitarian position is effective for many Christians, but not for others.

Binitarianism

Binitarianism lacks the simple logic and rigid consistency found in Unitarianism. It prides itself upon nuance and subtlety. This constitutes a weakness.

All the pegs upon which Binitarianism (and Trinitarianism in terms of the deity of Jesus) hangs its hat end up speculative at best and "iffy" at worst.

Since the notion of vicarious atonement is at the heart of the matter, evidence that calls this doctrine into question seriously weakens the Binitarian position. One such piece of evidence, and a large piece at that, is the theory of evolution.[2] Without an initial or first Adam, the notion and logic of a second Adam crumbles (see Romans 5:15-21 and 1 Corinthians 15:21-22). The whole concept of blood atonement is arguably a vestige of primitive aversive magic.[3]

The underlying principle that "only God can fully reveal God" also is open to criticism. One might concede the truth of the principle but then ask this question: What good is it for "God to reveal God" when the recipients of the revelation are mere mortals? Aren't we all subject to limited and often distorted perspectives, even when, objectively, the information we have been given is absolutely true?

Binitarianism, as previously argued, appeals to early Christian practices of ritual, worship, and song. Should dogmatic conclusions be drawn from such practices? Should a "mutation" in Jewish monotheism be extracted from reflection upon these practices? Incorporating a "second person" into the Godhead is serious business. Many Christian thinkers (Paul of Samosata; Lucian of Antioch; Arius of Alexandria; Eusebius of Nicomedia) objected to the "Church's" move in this direction. Binitarianism, it seems, bases its teachings not on the clear teaching of scripture, but upon retrojecting back into scripture speculations about Jesus' status that clearly were not evident in the teachings of Jesus or the Apostles. The Binitarian position should be approached with caution.

Trinitarianism

The critique just provided for the Binitarian view simply needs to be extended one step further for the Trinitarian view. The critical matter under dispute here is the status of the Spirit. Again, a complex of underlying principles and interpretive perspectives are called upon to provide warrant for the deification of the Spirit. But the price paid is too high. The simplicity, clarity, and consistency found in the Unitarian approach is set aside for the sake of a dogma that may lend itself to a mystification of the relevant data rather than to a clarification of the relevant data.

Consider the maze of terminology employed by Trinitarians. When I lecture on the Trinity in my undergraduate classes, I spend at least two hours laboring over the history, meaning, and evolution of meaning of the following, mostly Latin or Greek, terms: ousia; substantia; essentia; prosopon; persona; hypostasis; individium; subsistentia; modus subsistentia; perichoresis; circumincessio; schesis; homousia; homoiousia (note the one iota difference!); consubstantia; hypostatic union; theotokos; ekporeusis; processio; gennesia; spiration; filiation; substance and accidens; kenosis; in esse; ad extra; essentialiter; and personaliter.[4] Allow me to briefly comment on two sets of terms, ousia/hypostasis, and homousia/homoiousia. This will illustrate a major obstacle to the acceptance of the dogma of the Trinity.

The Greek word ousia is the noun form of the Greek verb "to be," conjugated as "I am," "you are," or "he, she, or it is." Hence, it refers to "being," or the "act of being." Thus, it points to the core essence of what a thing is (which in God's case is "isness," or "being"). The Greek word hypostasis is composed of two roots, hypo and stasis. Hypo basically means below or under. Stasis basically means to stand or remain. Thus, hypostasis refers to "that which stands or remains under." It, therefore, can and did refer to the same reality that ousia referred to, the essence of a thing, or the act of being. Ousia and hypostasis at one time were synonyms. But the logic of the Trinity required terminology that would service the need to make a distinction between the oneness and unity of God and the threeness and diversity within God. Ousia was designated to account for the former, hypostasis for the latter. Hypostasis took on the meaning "an individual instance of an essence." Thus, in Trinitarian thought, the Father, Son, and Spirit were considered three distinct hypostases. But, together, in their interrelatedness (the terms perichoresis or circumincessio are used here), they constitute the one ousia that is God. I hesitate to digress much further as my point is not to try to explain the concept of the Trinity. What I am attempting to point out is that, due to the difficulty, if not impossibility, of explaining the concept, Christian theologians were forced to assign new meanings or nuances to words that did not have these meanings or nuances prior to the introduction of the concept of the Trinity.[5] Is this how God reveals himself, through the messy, complicated wrangling of abstract terms? Perhaps. But one can hopefully see why many (Unitarian Christians) object, insisting that the simplicity of the gospel has been forfeited.

The other set of terms selected for comment is homousia and homoiousia. The Greek homo, means same (or like). The Greek homoi, means like (not same). We just explained ousia. Hence, the term refers to "that which is the same or like substance with another." In Trinitarian discussion, these words serviced the discussion of how the Son is to be related to the Father. Although not a term found in the Bible, theologians suggested the term to get at the proper Father-Son relationship. Trinitarians pushed for the term homousia, emphasizing the nuance of "same" rather than "like." Thus, the Nicene creed could go on and express this meaning with the phrases, "light of light, true God of true God, begotten not made, of one substance (homousia) with the Father." This way of putting things established, in the mind of Trinitarian interpreters, the complete deity of Jesus. But objectors to this interpretation (and there were many) insisted that if the nuance of "like" were allowed for the correct understanding of the term, which at one time was a possible nuance, they would be satisfied. Jesus could be "like" God, but God (the Father) would retain right of privilege as the supreme deity. The objectors suggested the term homoiousia, but it was rejected by the majority of the council. The little iota ("i" in Greek) mattered a lot. Again, with the evident invention of, or manipulation of, meanings and nuances of Greek words, one might hesitate or pause when considering their adopted meanings as God's revelation. Consider this comment by Hanson:

> people holding different views were using the same words as those who opposed them, but, unawares, giving them different meanings from those applied to them by those opponents.[6]

When one adds the previous objections mentioned regarding the Trinity (no clear statement of the Trinity in scripture; no polemic regarding deity of Spirit in the early Church; no evident worship of or prayer directed to the Spirit in the early Church) to the terminological objections just discussed, the plausibility of this dogma weakens.

A Reiteration of the Non-Sectarian Position

The human mind abhors uncertainty. Therefore, sincere Christians "favor" one or the other of the first three views set forth in this book. Each view can be defended from scripture, tradition, and select interpretive principles. Yet, each view can be challenged and critiqued if not deconstructed. Often an appeal is made to "faith," at least in the sense that one must exercise faith when reason falls short of its mark. I certainly agree. But one might just as well decide to exercise faith in this conclusion: God was not interested in human beings coming to such a precise understanding of his revelation; else the revelation would have been clearer. Perhaps God is not interested in creeds, or in being contained in a confessional box. Creeds and confessions are poor substitutes for an authentic relationship. They often are more about fear and control than love and living.

"Faith" often collapses from an authentic trust in an inexplicable higher power that is benevolent toward us (its primary meaning) to a mere conformity to the "correct" creed of the social group that one "wants" to belong to or at least feels the need to belong to. These considerations point a thinking person in the direction of the Non-Sectarian position.

Notes

1. The history on this is not pleasant, and censorship and suppression of views works both ways. See Helen Ellerbe, *The Dark Side of Christianity* (Orlando: Morningstark & Lark, 1995), 14-29, and Richard E. Rubenstein, *When Jesus Became God: The Epic Fight over Christ's Divinity in the Last Days of Rome* (New York: Harcourt Brace, 1999), 57-58.

2. I am using the word "theory" here, not in its popular sense as something contrary to "fact," but in its scientific sense as a collection of confirmed hypotheses awaiting falsification.

3. For a discussion of the applicability of aversive magic to sacrifice, see David Noss, *A History of the World's Religions* (Upper Saddle River: Prentice Hall, 1999, tenth edition), 16-17.

4. Helpful discussions of the history, meaning, and usage of these essential terms to Trinitarian discussion may be found in Richard A. Muller, *Dictionary of Latin and Greek Theological Terms* (Grand Rapids: Baker, 1995).

5. A thorough discussion and documentation of the history and ambiguity of these terms is provided by R. P. C. Hanson, *The Search for the Christian Doctrine of God* (Edinburgh: T & T Clark, 1988), 181-203.

6. *Ibid.*, 181.

Conclusion

Four Models for understanding the H/holy S/spirit have been set forth, defined and defended in light of biblical passages and select interpretive principles. We have seen, especially with Chapter One's Preliminary Illustrations, wide divergence among 25 representative English translations. There seems to be little commitment to, consistency with, or clarity regarding a given Model. This is especially evident in the oscillations between upper casing and lower casing S/spirit.

Chapters Two through Five presented first a brief summary of the position of a given Model, then an expansion of the arguments. No doubt some important passages were overlooked. Perhaps some passages were improperly or inadequately analyzed. Certainly, some significant interpretive principles were neglected. Yet, the portrayal of the general lines of argumentation for each of the Four Models in a positive and persuasive manner seems achieved. Hopefully, readers sense a balance or evenness in my treatment of the pros and the cons for each Model.

It's difficult for me to declare my preference for one Model over another (this admission *almost* forces me into the Non-Sectarian Model). Readers may also find it difficult to state their preference. Several outcomes of this study are hoped for: mutual understanding, growth in humility, commitment to continued study, and a willingness to dialogue with those with whom we may disagree.

The Christian Church, throughout its history, has had a difficult time realizing her Lord's vision of unity (John 17:20-21). I do think that unity in doctrine and dogma is an ideal all Christians should strive for. I also think that unity in love and respect for one another, despite essential differences, serves as a worthy option when the former seems unattainable. It certainly might help open doors to future possibilities of a doctrinal unity. If this book contributes in any meaningful manner to any of my readers in achieving either of these goals, I will feel gratified that my labors were not in vain.

My beloved grandmother (Isabel Blume; 1901-1993) often reminded me that "above all doctrine, belief, and creed stands the Christ who meets our need."

Illustration 1

God as Father

Four Models

(1) In relation to the divine nature of the Son:

(2) In relation to the human nature of the Son:

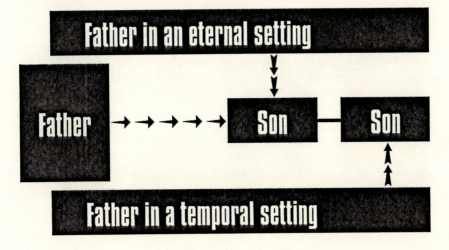

Illustration 1

Four Models (continued)

(3) In relation to creation, as the Father distinct from Son and Spirit:

(4) In relation to creation, as the one Triune God:

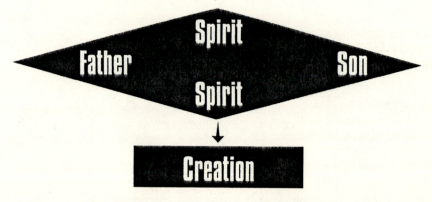

Illustration 2

The Unitarian Model

Only the Father is God

The Father gives
↓
holy spirit
↓
to believers in OT

The Father gives
↓
holy spirit
↓
to Jesus while on earth

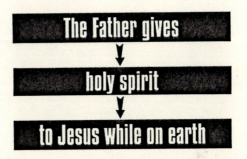

The Father and the risen Jesus give
↓
holy spirit
↓
to Jesus' followers

Illustration 3

The Binitarian Model

The Father and the Son are God, one God, two persons

Illustration 4

The Trinitarian Model

The Father, Son and Holy Spirit are one God, three persons

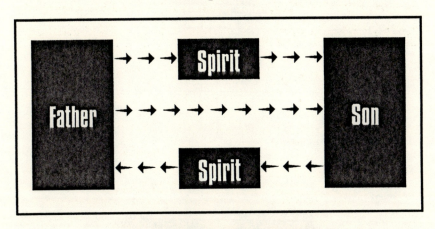

Illustration 5

The personification and hypostatization revelation matrix

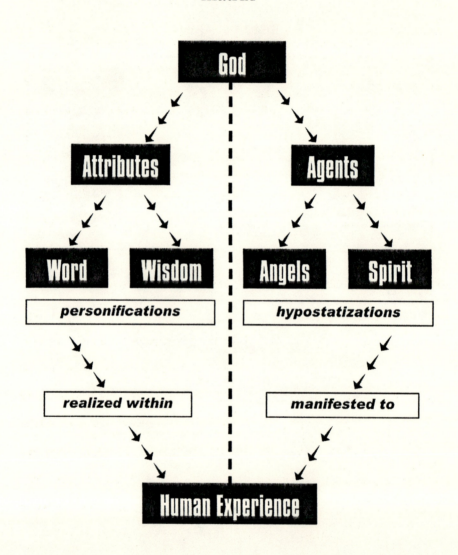

Bibliography

———. *The Catechism of the Catholic Church*. Ligouri: LigouriPublications, 1994.

———. *Englishman's Hebrew and Chaldee Concordance*. Grand Rapids: Zondervan, 1970.

Aglen, A. S. "Lord." Pp. 137 in *Hastings Dictionary of the Bible*, Vol. 3, James Hastings ed. New York: Charles Scribner's Sons, 1963.

Arndt, W. F. and F. W. Gingrich. *A Greek-English Lexicon of the New Testament*, 2nd edition, revised by Frederick W. Danker. Chicago: Univ. of Chicago Press, 1979.

Bietenhard, Hans. "Lord." Pp. 510-19 in *New International Dictionary of the New Testament*, Volume 2, Colin Brown, ed. Grand Rapids: Eerdmans, 1976-78.

Beilby, James K. & Paul R. Eddy. *Divine Foreknowledge: 4 Views*. Downers Grove: Intervarsity, 2001.

Bercot, David W, ed. *A Dictionary of Christian Beliefs*. Peabody: Hendrickson, 1998.

Blomberg, Craig. *Matthew: The New American Commentary*, Volume 22. Nashville: Broadman, 1992.

Braumann, G. "Advocate, Paraclete, Helper." Pp. 88-91 in *The New International Dictionary of New Testament Theology*, Vol 1, Grand Rapids: Zondervan, 1975.

Brown, Colin, ed. *New International Dictionary of the New Testament*, 3 vols. Grand Rapids: Eerdmans, 1976-78.

Brown, Francis, S. R. Driver, and Charles A. Briggs. *A Hebrew and English Lexicon of the Old Testament*, rev. ed. Oxford: Clarendon, 1972.

Brown, Raymond E. *The Gospel According to John*. 2 Vols. Garden City: Doubleday, 1966.

———. *Jesus God and Man: Modern Biblical Reflections*. New York: MacMillan, 1967.

———. *The Birth of the Messiah*. Garden City: Doubleday, 1977.

———. *Introduction to the New Testament: Anchor Bible Reference Library*. New York: Doubleday, 1997.

Brown, Tricia Gates. *Spirit in the Writings of John: Johannine Pneumatology in Social-Scientific Perspective*. London: T & T Clark, 2003.

Bruce, F. F. *The Epistle to the Hebrews: The New International Commentary on The New Testament*. Grand Rapids: Michigan, 1964.

Bruner, Frederick Dale. *A Theology of the Holy Spirit: The Pentecostal Witness and the New Testament Witness*. Grand Rapids: Eerdmans, 1970.

——— & William E. Hordern. *The Holy Spirit, The Shy Member of the Trinity*. Minneapolis: Augsburg, 1984.

Bullinger, E. W. *Figures of Speech Used in the Bible*. Grand Rapids: Baker. 1968 (reprint of 1898 original).

Charlesworth, James H. *The Old Testament Pseudepigrapha*, Volume 2. New York: Doubleday, 1985.

Clouse, Robert G, ed. *The Meaning of the Millennium: Four Views*. Downers Grove: Intervarsity, 1977.

Crockett, William, ed. *Four Views on Hell*. Grand Rapids: Zondervan, 1992.

Dana, H.E. & Julius Mantey. *A Manual Grammar of the Greek New Testament*. Toronto: MacMillan, 1955.

Danielou, Alain. *Yoga*. Rochester: Inner Traditions International, 1991.

deJonge, Marinus. *Christology in Context: The Earliest Response to Jesus*. Philadelphia: Westminster, 1988.
Delitzsch, Franz. *Commentary on the Epistle to the Hebrews*, 2 vols. Minneapolis: Klock & Klock,1978 (reprint of 1871 original).
Dunn, J. D. G. *Christology in the Making*. Philadelphia: Westminster, 1980.
Ellerbe, Helen. *The Dark Side of Christian History*. Orlando: Morningstark & Lark, 1995.
Erickson, Millard J. *God in Three Persons: A Contemporary Interpretation of the Trinity*. Grand Rapids: Baker, 1995.
Fideler, David. *Jesus Christ Sun of God: Ancient Cosmology and Early Christian Symbolism*. Wheaton: Quest Books, 1993.
Forestall, J. T. "Proverbs." Pp. 495-505 in *The Jerome Biblical Commentary*. R. E. Brown, J. A. Fitzmeyer & R. E. Murphy, eds. Englewood Cliffs: Prentice Hall, 1968.
Funk, Robert & Roy Hoover, eds. *The Five Gospels*. New York: MacMillan, 1993.
Gelpi, Donald L. *The Divine Mother: A Trinitarian Theology of the Holy Spirit*. Lanham: University Press of America, 1984.
Goodrick, Edward W. *Do It Yourself Hebrew and Greek: Everybody's Guide to the Language Tools*. Grand Rapids: Zondervan, 1976.
Goodspeed, Edgar J. *The Apostolic Fathers*. New York: Harper & Brothers, 1950.
Grant, Robert M. *Gods and the One God*. Philadelphia: Westminster, 1986.
————. *The Early Christian Doctrine of God*. Charlottesville: University Press of Virginia, 1966,
Grillmeyer, Aloys. (translated by J. S. Bowden). *Christ in Christian Tradition: From the Apostolic Age to Chalcedon*. New York: Sheed and Ward, 1965.
Harris, Murray J. *Jesus as God: The New Testament Use of Theos in Reference to Jesus*. Grand Rapids: Baker, 1992.
Hanson, R.P.C. *The Search for the Christian Doctrine of God*. Edinburgh. T & T Clark, 1988.
Harvey, A. E. *Jesus and the Constraints of History*. Philadelphia: Westminster, 1982.
Henderson, J. B. *The Construction of Orthodoxy and Heresy: Neo-Confucianism, Islamic, Jewish, and Early Christian Patterns*. Albany: State University of New York, 1988.
Hinnells. R. *Penguin Dictionary of Religion*. London: Penguin Books, 1995.
Hooker, S. H. "The Spirit Was Not Yet." Pp 372-80 in *New Testament Studies* 9, 1962.
Horn, F. W. "Holy Spirit." Pp 275-80 in *The Anchor Bible Dictionary*, ed. David Noel Freedman et al. New York: Doubleday, 1992.
Hurtado, Larry W. *At the Origins of Christian Worship: The Context and Character of Earliest Christian Devotion*. Grand Rapids: Eerdmans, 1999.
————. *One God, One Lord: Early Christian Devotion and Ancient Monotheism*. Minneapolis: Fortress, 2003.
————. *How on Earth Did Jesus Become a God? Historical Questions about Earliest Devotion to Jesus*. Grand Rapids: Eerdmans, 2005.
Kohlenberger, John R. III, ed. *The Precise Parallel New Testament*. New York: Oxford University, 1995.
Lightfoot, J. B. *Saint Paul's Epistles to the Colossians and to Philemon*. Grand Rapids: Zondervan, 1976 (reprint of revised 1879 edition).
Malina, Bruce J. & Richard L. Rohrbaugh. *Social-Science Commentary on the Synoptic Gospels*. Minneapolis: Fortress, 1992.

Bibliography

McCready, Douglas. *He Came Down from Heaven: The Pre-existence of Christ and the Christian Faith.* Downers Grove: Intervarsity Press, 2005.

McDonnell, Killian. *The Other Hand of God: The Holy Spirit as the Universal Touch and Goal.* Minnesota: Liturgical Press Collegeville, 2003.

Montague, George. 1976. *The Holy Spirit: The Growth of a Biblical Tradition: A Commentary on the Principal Texts of the Old and New Testaments*: New York: Paulist, 1976.

Moore, Rebecca. *Voices of Christianity: A Global Introduction.* Boston: McGraw Hill, 2006.

Muller, Richard A. *Dictionary of Latin and Greek Theological Terms.* Grand Rapids: Baker, 1995.

Noss, David. (Tenth edition). *A History of the World's Religions.* Upper Saddle River: Prentice Hall, 1999.

Pelikan, Jaroslav. *The Christian Tradition: A History of the Development of Doctrine, Volume 1.* Chicago: Chicago University Press, 1971.

Ringgren, Helmer. *Word and Wisdom: Studies in the Hypostatization of Divine Qualities and Functions.* Lund: H Ohlsson's boktr, 1947.

Robinson, James M., Paul Hoffman, and John S. Kloppenborg, eds. *The Sayings Gospel Q in Greek and English with Parallels form the Gospels of Mark and Thomas.* Minneapolis: Fortress, 2002.

Rubenstein, Richard E. *When Jesus Became God: The Epic Fight over Christ's Divinity in the Last Days of Rome.* New York: Harcourt Brace, 1999.

Schaberg, Jane. *The Father, The Son, and The Holy Spirit: SBL Dissertation Series 61.* Chico: Scholars Press, 1982.

Schnackenburg, Rudolf. *The Gospel according to John*, Volume 1. New York: Herder & Herder, 1968.

Segal, A. F. *Two Powers in Heaven: Early Rabbinic Reports about Christianity and Gnosticism.* Leiden: Brill, 1977.

Spronk, K. "Lord." Pp. 531-33 in Karel van der Toorn, Bob Becking & Peter W. van derHorst, eds. *Dictionary of Deities and Demons in the Bible.* Grand Rapids: Eerdmans, 1999.

Stafford, Greg. *JW's Defended: An Answer to Scholars and Critics*: Second Edition: Huntington Beach: Elihu Books, 2000.

Strong, James, ed. *The Exhaustive Concordance of the Bible.* Nashville: Abingdon, 1979.

Underhill, Evelyn. *Mysticism: The Nature and Development of Spiritual Consciousness.* Oxford: Oneworld, 2004 (reprint of 1910 original).

VonRad, Gerhard. *Genesis.* Philadelphia: Westminster, 1961.

VonWahlde, Urban C. *The Earliest Version of John's Gospel. Recovering the Gospel of Signs.* Wilmington: Michael Glazier, 1989.

Wierwille, Victor Paul. *Receiving the Holy Spirit Today.* New Knoxville: The Way, 1967.

Wigoner, Geoffry, "Holy Spirit." Pp. 190 in *The Encyclopedia of the Jewish Religion.* RJ Zwi Werblowsky, ed. New York: Aduma Books, 1986.

Wright, J. Stafford. "God." Pp. 66-85 in *The New International Dictionary of New Testament Theology, Vol. 2* (editor: Colin Brown). Grand Rapids: Zondervan, 1976.

Author Index

Aglen, A. S., 34
Arndt, W. F., 34
Bietenhard, Hans, 22, 33, 34
Beilby, James K., xi
Bercot, David W., 57
Blomberg, Craig, 35
Briggs, Charles A., 17, 49
Braumann, G., 50
Brown, Colin, 33
Brown, Francis, 17, 49
Brown, R.E., 33, 35, 48
Brown, Tricia Gates, 50
Bruce, F. F., xix
Bruner, Frederick Dale, 35
Bullinger, E. W., 35
Charlesworth, James H., 34
Clouse, Robert G., xi
Crockett, William, xi
Dana, H.E., 49
Danielou, Alain, 58
Delitzsch, Franz, xix,
Driver, S. R., 17, 49
Dunn, J. D. G., 54
Eddy, Paul R., xi
Ellerbe, Helen, 63
Erickson, Millard J., 34
Fideler, David, 57
Fitzmeyer, J. A., 48
Forestall, J. T., 48
Funk, Robert, 31
Gelpi, Donald L., xviii, 57
Gingrich, F. W., 34
Goodrick, Edward W., xix, 35
Goodspeed, Edgar J., xix, 35
Grant, Robert, 34, 49
Grillmeyer, Aloys, 49
Harris, Murray J., 49
Hanson, R.P.C., 17, 33, 35, 58, 63, 64
Harvey, A. E., 34
Henderson, J. B., 33
Hinnells. R., xi
Hoffman, Paul, 36
Hooker, S. H., 50
Hoover, Roy, 31
Horn, F. W., xix
Hordern, William E., 35

Hurtado, Larry W., 33, 49, 57
Kohlenberger, John R. III, 33, 34
Lightfoot, J. B., 49
Malina, Bruce, 22, 34
Mantey, Julius, 49
McCready, Douglas, 17
McDonnell, Killian, 35
Moore, Rebecca, 57
Muller, Richard A., 64
Murphey, R. E., 48
Noss, David, 64
Pelikan, Jaroslav, 35
Rinnggren, Helmer, 50
Robinson, James M., 36
Rohrbaugh, Richard L., 24, 34
Rubenstein, Richard E., 63
Schaberg, Jane, 35
Schnackenburg, Rudolph, 34
Segal, A. F., 49
Spronk, K., 34
Stafford, Greg, 33
Strong, James, 49
Underhill, Evelyn, 17
VonRad, Gerhard, 17
VonWahlde, Urban C., 50
Wigoner, Geoffry, 33
Wright, J. Stafford, 33

Scripture Index

First Testament

Reference   *Page*

Genesis
1:2	1, 15
1:3	1
1:11	2
1:12	2
1:20	2
1:21	2
1:24	2
1:26	2
3:8	2
3:22	60
6:3	2, 15
6:17	17
7:15	17
7:22	17
8:1	17
17:7	55
26:25	17
41:8	3, 15
41:25	4
41:38	3, 4

Exodus
4:16	27, 34
28:3	4, 5, 16
31:3	4, 5, 16
33:1-2	12
33:2	12
33:14	12

Numbers
11:11-12	6
11:16-17	5, 6
11:17	16
11:25-31	5, 6, 16
11:26	15

Deuteronomy
6:4	23

2 Kings
2:9-15	48

Psalms
45:7	27
51:9-12	7, 15, 16
51:10-12	8
51:13	33
82:6	27, 34
104:4	xvi
136:12	57

Proverbs
8:22	26
8:22-23	38

Ecclesiates
9:5	60

Wisdom
9:1	57

Sirach
42:15	57

Isaiah
7:14	8
9:1-6	8
11:1-2	8
11:2	15
40:13	9, 10, 16
42:1	8, 46
42:8	33
44:3	17
48:16	11, 18, 16
55:11	57
63:9-11	12, 13
63:10	12, 13, 14, 15, 33
63:11	12, 13, 14, 35

Jeremiah
10:12	57
31:31-34	46

Ezekiel
36:25-27	46
36:26-27	13, 15
36:27	16

Daniel
7:13-14   35

Joel
3:1-3   17
3:5   42

Second Testament

Matthew
1:19   30
1:20   30
1:19-20   31
3:11   30, 31, 32
ch. 5-8   59
5:17-20   30
7:11   30, 31
7:21-23   60
10:1   47
10:5-6   30
10:20   47
11:14   48
11:27   48
12:31-32   30, 31
15:1-10   30
23:1-13   30
23:9-10   48
24:36   31
28:18-20   44, 57
28:19   30, 31, 32, 48

Mark
2:21-22   54
6:13   47
6:15   48
8:38   31
9:4   60
10:17   24
10:18   24
10:45   37
13:11   47
13:32   25

Luke
1:15   47
1:17   47
1:35   33
1:41   47
1:67   47

2:25-27   47
2:38   47
3:15   32
7:1-10   44
7:5   44
7:6   44
7:9-10   45
11:13   31, 47

John
1:1-5   55
1:1   27, 33, 38, 39, 45, 48
1:14   33, 38, 45
1:18   27, 33, 38, 40, 41, 45, 48
1:21   48
1:30   33
1:32-33   46, 47
3:1-5   46
3:1-7   46
3:5-8   47
3:13   33, 38
3:16-18   33
3:16   41
3:17   47
3:31   33
3:34   45, 47
3:36   45
4:11   45
4:20-24   46
4:23-24   47
4:24   46
4:25   45
5:19-26   45
5:23   48
5:24   60
5:26   48
6:35   45
6:38   25
6:41   33
6:48   33
6:51   33
6:63   47
7:28   33
7:37-39   45, 46, 47, 54
7:39   47

Scripture Index

8:12	45	2:36	23
8:14-19	48	2:38	31, 43
8:23-24	33	5:3-4	44
8:29	48	7:59-60	42
8:36	33	ch. 8	29
8:42	33	8:9-25	27, 29
8:58	33, 55	8:13	28
9:39-41	47	8:16	31, 43
10:7	45	8:20-23	35
10:11	45	8:20	28
10:15	48	8:26-40	35
10:30	45, 48	ch.10	29
10:34	34	10:48	31, 43
10:34-35	27	13:2	44, 57
10:38	33	15:1	55
11:25	45	15:28	44, 57
ch 14-16	26	ch.19	29
14:1	45, 48	19:5	31, 43
14:3	60	22:16	31
14:6	33, 45, 47, 48		
14:8	45	**Romans**	
14:9	47	1:7	48
14:10	48	3:25	37
14:16	44, 47, 57	3:27-28	60
14:17	26, 47	5:5	55
14:20	47	5:8	41
14:26	44, 45, 47, 57	5:15-21	61
15:1	48	6:3	43
15:26	44	8:4-6	27
16:7	44, 57	8:9	55
16:8-11	47	8:11-16	27
16:13-15	45	8:16	57
16:13	25, 48	8:26-27	44
16:14	45	8:26	27, 44
16:28	33	9:5	27
17:1-5	22, 33, 38	10:9-10	42
17:1	22	10:13	42
17:3	22	15:6	22
17:5	22, 39, 55	16:27	48
17:20-21	65		
19:30	46, 54	**1 Corinthians**	
20:21	46	1:3	48
20:22	46, 48	ch. 2	10
20:28	27	2:7	9
		2:10-14	11
Acts		2:10-16	10, 57
2:4	29	2:11	15
2:17-21	17	2:12	15, 27

Scripture Index

2:13	15
2:16	9
6:11	27
8:1-13	22
8:4	22
8:5	22, 23
8:6	22, 23
8:8	23
10:18	43
10:22	43
11:3	23
12:3	27, 55
12:4-6	48
15:21-22	61
15:24-28	23
15:28	23, 48
16:22	42

2 Corinthians
1:2	48
1:3	26
3:17	57
4:4	27
5:1-2	60
11:31	26
12:8-9	42
13:14	32, 44, 48, 57

Galatians
3:1-5	57
3:3	27
4:6	27, 55, 57

Ephesians
1:2	48
1:3	21, 26
1:13	57
1:17	26
2:8	60
2:13	55
2:18	27, 56
3:1-6	55
4:1-30	30
4:3	22
4:4-6	21, 48, 57
4:11-32	22
4:30	30, 44, 57
6:23	48

Philippians
1:2	48
1:21-23	60
2:6-11	23
2:9	23
3:3	27

Colossians
1:2	48
1:15	26, 38

1 Thessalonians
1:3	48
3:11	41

2 Thessalonians
1:2	48
1:7-8	31
2:16-17	41

1 Timothy
1:2	48
2:5	32, 48
2:6	37
5:21	31
6:16	60

2 Timothy
1:2	48

Titus
1:4	48
2:13	27

Philemon
3	48

Hebrews
1:1-2	38, 39, 40, 41, 42, 47, 48, 54
1:8	27
9:14	48, 57
10:26-31	60
13:20-21	48

James
1:1	48
2:8	60

2:18   60

1 Peter
1:2   48
1:3   26, 48
4:17-18 60
5:10   48

2 Peter
1:1-2   48
1:1   27

1 John
1:3   48
2:2   37
3:24   55
4:10   37, 41
4:13-14 48
4:13-15 27
5:1   48
5:20   27

2 John
1:3   48

Jude
1   48

Revelation
1:1-2   31
1:6   26
3:5   31
3:14   26, 38
5:13   48
6:9   60
14:10   31
17:14   34
22:17   57

About the Author

Garrett Kenney is an assistant professor of English/Religious Studies at Eastern Washington University (EWU). He is currently the Program Advisor for the Religious Studies minor that is offered within the Humanities Program at Eastern. Dr. Kenney has taught for many years at various schools and colleges in the Spokane and Cheney area. In addition to his many years at EWU, Dr. Kenney also taught religion at Gonzaga Prep High School, Gonzaga University, and the Inland Empire School of the Bible.

Among other works, Professor Kenney is the author of: *Introduction to Religion* (Dubuque: Kendall/Hunt, 1988); *Lessons in Religion* (Dubuque: Kendall/Hunt, 1996); *Lessons and Lectures in Religion* (Dubuque: Kendall/Hunt, 2000); *John 1:1 as Proof Text:Trinitarian or Unitarian?* (Lanham: University Press of America, 1999); *The Relationship of Christology to Ethics in the First Epistle of John* (Lanham: University Press of America, 2000); and, *Leadership in John: An Analysis of the Situation and Strategy of Gospel and Epistles of John* (Lanham: University Press of America, 2000).